Editors' Preface to Macmillan Studies in Economics

The rapid growth of academic literature in the field of economics has posed serious problems for both students and teachers of the subject. The latter find it difficult to keep pace with more than few areas of the subject so that an inevitable trend towards specialism emerges. The student quickly loses perspective as the maze of theories and models grows, particularly at a time when so much reappraisal of the established paradigms is taking place.

The aim of the 'Macmillan Studies in Economics' is to offer students, and perhaps some teachers as well, short, reasonably critical overviews of developments in selected areas of economics, particularly those in which current controversies are to be found. As far as possible the titles have been selected to form an integrated whole, although inevitably whole areas have been neglected as being unsuited to the style, format and length of the titles in the series.

In some cases the volumes are rather more like essays than surveys. In most cases, however, the aim is to survey the salient literature in a critical fashion. The level of understanding required to read the volumes varies with the complexity of the subject, but they have been generally written to suit the second- and third-year undergraduate seeking to place his reading of the detailed literature in an over-all context. They are *not* textbooks. Instead they seek to give the kind of perspective that might well be lost by reading longer textbooks on their own, or by reading articles in journals. In particular, they should be most suited to pre-examination revision periods. They are not intended to substitute for the essential reading and assimilation of the original works that they seek to survey and assess.

MACMILLAN STUDIES IN ECONOMICS

General Editors: D. C. ROWAN and G. R. FISHER

Executive Editor: D. W. PEARCE

Published

John Burton: WAGE INFLATION
Ben Fine: MARX'S 'CAPITAL'
Douglas Fisher: MONETARY POLICY
Miles Fleming: MONETARY THEORY
C. J. Hawkins and D. W. Pearce: CAPITAL INVESTMENT APPRAISAL
C. J. Hawkins: THEORY OF THE FIRM
David F. Heathfield: PRODUCTION FUNCTIONS
Dudley Jackson: POVERTY
P. N. Junankar: INVESTMENT: THEORIES AND EVIDENCE
J. E. King: LABOUR ECONOMICS
John King and Philip Regan: RELATIVE INCOME SHARES
J. A. Kregel: THE THEORY OF ECONOMIC GROWTH
J. A. Kregel: THEORY OF CAPITAL
Richard Lecomber: ECONOMIC GROWTH VERSUS THE ENVIRONMENT
George McKenzie: THE MONETARY THEORY OF INTERNATIONAL TRADE
David J. Mayston: THE IDEA OF SOCIAL CHOICE
C. A. Nash: PUBLIC VERSUS PRIVATE TRANSPORT
S. K. Nath: A PERSPECTIVE OF WELFARE ECONOMICS
Antony Peaker: ECONOMIC GROWTH IN MODERN BRITAIN
D. W. Pearce: COST-BENEFIT ANALYSIS
Maurice Peston: PUBLIC GOODS AND THE PUBLIC SECTOR
Nicholas Rau: TRADE CYCLES: THEORY AND EVIDENCE
David Robertson: INTERNATIONAL TRADE POLICY
Charles K. Rowley: ANTITRUST AND ECONOMIC EFFICIENCY
C. H. Sharp: TRANSPORT ECONOMICS
G. K. Shaw: FISCAL POLICY
R. Shone: THE PURE THEORY OF INTERNATIONAL TRADE
M. J. Stabler: AGRICULTURAL ECONOMICS AND RURAL LAND-USE
Frank J. B. Stilwell: REGIONAL ECONOMIC POLICY
A. P. Thirlwall: FINANCING ECONOMIC DEVELOPMENT
John Vaizey: THE ECONOMICS OF EDUCATION
J. van Doorn: DISEQUILIBRIUM ECONOMICS
Peter A. Victor: ECONOMICS OF POLLUTION
Grahame Walshe: INTERNATIONAL MONETARY REFORM
Michael G. Webb: PRICING POLICIES OF THE PUBLIC ENTERPRISES
E. Roy Weintraub: CONFLICT AND CO-OPERATION IN ECONOMICS
E. Roy Weintraub: GENERAL EQUILIBRIUM THEORY

Forthcoming

R. W. Anderson: ECONOMICS OF CRIME
B. Morgan: MONETARISM AND KEYNESIANISM
F. Pennance: HOUSING ECONOMICS
A. Ziderman: MANPOWER TRAINING: THEORY AND POLICY

Theory of Capital

J. A. KREGEL

University of Southampton

© J. A. Kregel 1976

First published 1976 by
THE MACMILLAN PRESS LTD
London and Basingstoke
Associated companies in New York Dublin
Melbourne Johannesburg and Madras
SBN 333 16714 7

Printed in Great Britain by
THE ANCHOR PRESS LTD
Tiptree, Essex

Contents

Warnings and Acknowledgements

This is not a Modern Treatise on capital theory, nor is it a Compleat History of the Hundred Years War carried on by capital theorists. Instead it attempts to put the debates of the past twenty years into the perspective of the past 100 (and more), hoping thereby to explain the context and intention of the most recent skirmishes. It has become common for writers in the debates to make general, unreferenced statements about positions held and methods employed by previous writers and schools. The book attempts to bring some sense into these assessments (as well as encourage the reader to go back and look for himself!). The methods involved and the basic results of the 'Two Cambridges' debates are outlined to provide an introduction to a reading of the recent literature cited in the bibliography (Harcourt's excellent survey [29] makes presentation of more technical aspects unnecessary). The last chapter seeks to assess the contribution of the debates.

As capital theory has become associated with the theory of production and production functions, Heathfield's survey [36] of the subject provides a useful source for those in need of review. In addition, capital and growth theory have many aspects in common but I have attempted to avoid duplication with the earlier book on growth in this series [50]. The two books may be read as complements.

I should like to thank P. Garegnani, G. C. Harcourt and Ian Steedman, who all, directly or indirectly, entered into the production of this book by providing counsel or criticism. Had I heeded all the suggestions and advice offered the above named would be wholly responsible for any misinterpretation or error. Since I did not, they are not.

                                                                J.A.K.

1 Introduction

The general validity of Keynes's critique of orthodox economic theory is still an unsettled question (as is the question of what the critique actually comprises) amongst economists. There can be little question, however, that the appearance of the *General Theory* [48] did much to change the focal point of theoretical economic enquiry; the questions that were posed and the framework that was used to analyse them. One set of problems that virtually disappeared from academic discussion as a result of this change of emphasis was the analysis of capital and capital accumulation – questions upon which economists had been in active theoretical dispute almost since the inception of abstract economic reasoning.

This rather sudden and enduring (almost twenty years) disappearance is most paradoxical for Keynes did offer an alternative approach to capital theory, albeit in a context totally different from the previous debates which he found of little use [48 pp. 138–40]. On the other hand, the Keynesian setting of the short period with a given stock of productive equipment diverted interest away from the analysis of capital accumulation; while a theory of interest based on liquidity preference in a monetary-production economy seemed to rule out the discussion of interest as the return to capital.

Keynes enforced this difficulty by rejecting outright both the usefulness and the theoretical possibility of talking about, measuring or comparing capital at different points in time. These objections were bound up in Keynes's critique of the use and measure of 'real income' (i.e. income in physical not value terms after deduction of physical input costs) in orthodox theory. In Keynes's view it was illegitimate to talk of the real income of the community for 'the community's output of goods and services is a non-homogeneous complex which cannot be measured, strictly speaking, except in certain special cases, as for example when all the items of one output are included in the same proportions in another output' [48 p. 38], i.e. Keynes is arguing that diverse physical outputs cannot be combined in a meaningful single-valued physical aggregate, except in the special case (cf. p. 67, below) where all outputs have other outputs as inputs and each output requires these inputs in the same proportions.

Further, the measure of net output will contain, as well as goods and services, an increment or decrement of capital goods in excess or shortfall of the replacement of equipment wearing out in the current period, i.e. a net increase or decrease in the stock of productive equipment. One then has to measure the total increase in real capital equipment and measure the wastage to be deducted from this quantity to find the net real accumulation of productive equipment that is to be included under 'real income'. 'But,' Keynes objects, 'since this deduction is not a deduction in terms of money . . . [one] is involved in assuming that there can be a change in physical quantity, although there has been no physical change, i.e. . . . [one] is covertly introducing changes in *value*' [48 pp. 38–9].

Keynes thus argues that 'until a satisfactory system of units has been adopted' the precise definition of net capital output 'is an impossible task'. 'The problem of comparing one real output with another and of then calculating net output by setting off new items of equipment against wastage of old items presents conundrums which permit, one can confidently say, of no solution' [48 p. 39]. Keynes then goes on to propose the use of 'two fundamental units of quantity, namely, quantities of money value and quantities of employment' (wage-units) [48 p. 41], to which he later adds a third unit, time [48 p. 214], all of which are homogeneous for aggregate analysis.

It is my belief that much unnecessary perplexity can be avoided if we limit ourselves strictly to the two units, money and labour, when we are dealing with the behaviour of the economic system as a whole; reserving the use of units of particular outputs and equipments to the occasions when we are analysing the output of individual firms or industries in isolation; and the use of vague concepts, such as the quantity of output as a whole, the quantity of capital equipment as a whole and the general level of prices to the occasions when we are attempting some historical comparison which is within certain (perhaps fairly wide) limits avowedly imprecise and approximate [48 p. 43];

8

(such comparisons Keynes likened to the possibility of deciding whether 'Queen Victoria was a better Queen but not a happier woman than Queen Elizabeth' [48 p. 40]).

It is not surprising that such views put to rest the continuing debate over capital which had been described in an article published at about the same time, as 'to show that "capital" is a distinct factor of production, which can be measured in homogeneous units, both in the production of particular goods and in the economic system as a whole; that the price of this factor is the rate of interest; and that both capital and interest can thus be brought into the framework of production and distribution theory on the same plane as "labour" and "land" ' [45 p. 192] (a less extreme exposition of the same propositions is [35]). Except for notable exceptions, Keynes's theory brushed the 'vague concept' of capital, along with the more general problems of value and distribution, into a corner and replaced them with concerns over the determination of the volume of employment and money G.N.P. in a short-period situation in which given productive capacity could be more or less intensively used.

One notable exception was Harrod, who objected not to the restriction of Keynes's analysis to the short period, but to the static character of the approach. Soon after the basic outlines of Keynes's theory became known, Harrod was taken with the idea that the requirements of full employment in a static, given period of time might be in contradiction with the main-tenance of full employment over time in a dynamic system. Harrod thus sought to rework Keynes's system in dynamic terms. What bothered Harrod was that a full-employment posi-tion which required positive amounts of net saving and investment implied a change in the stock of productive capacity between the present period and future periods when the positive investment emerged as new machinery. Would the current relation of saving and investment which gave full employment in the current period with the current given stock of productive capacity also produce full employment in the next period with an increased amount of capacity? Would there be too little capital to give employment to all those seeking work, or would there be too much, leaving capitalists with excess capacity which might lead them to decrease their investment

9

plans and thus reduce aggregate demand and employment?

To start to answer these questions it was necessary to know the relation between money investment and the future productive capacity that it would produce, as well as the capacity of the future stock of capital to provide employment, i.e. the proportion in which labour and productive capacity could combine to produce output, for the concern of the capitalist investors was the relation of their future productive capacity to their expected sales in the future. Harrod tried to embody these relationships in the concept of the 'capital coefficient' [34 p. 22] which relates the money costs of investment in new productive capacity to the money flow of output that it could produce under normal conditions of utilisation. In fact, Harrod includes in his concept of capital, not only what one would think of as capital goods proper, but the value of all goods and services that may be required to produce an additional unit of money sales.

Up to this point, Harrod's dynamic extension of Keynes's theory is well within the strictures made by Keynes concerning the use of 'units' for the purposes of measurement. Despite Harrod's careful definitions and the necessity of following them (thus dynamic does not mean 'long period' and does not imply comparisons nor change over time, but simply the use of rates of change at a point of time; and the 'capital coefficient' does not relate to the production relations between physical capital goods, labour and the output produced from fixed or variable combinations of the two, cf. [34, 17]) his capital coefficient was soon translated into a 'capital–output' ratio in physical units, and his dynamic theory was taken to be a long-period analogue to Keynes's short-period approach.

However, once these seemingly innocent misinterpretations of Harrod were made they instantly gave rise to those 'vague concepts' and comparisons that Keynes had sought to banish from aggregate economics, and, not unexpectedly, soon generated the current disputes over the theory of capital which Harcourt in his survey [27] has called 'Some Cambridge controversies in the theory of capital'. Since the debates represent, in a sense, a return to previous questions that were in dispute throughout the last quarter of the nineteenth and first third of the twentieth centuries the historical evolution of the

10

theory will be briefly surveyed in Chapter 2 to allow us to gain a better appreciation of the current positions. The fact that many economists were willing to re-open discussion of capital in a context that had been almost untouched for twenty years gives witness to the degree to which Keynes influenced the direction of economic analysis. The way in which the discussions were re-introduced, however, says little for the enduring influence of his ideas, at any rate where capital and its measurement were concerned.

On the other hand, while the theoretical debates about capital continued throughout the early periods of the twentieth century, some economists were turning to the application of statistical methods to economic problems. These applications, which have developed into what is now known as econometrics, were less concerned with theoretical debate than with attempts to 'test' various theoretical relations, suitably adapted to available data. One of the earliest studies was Moore's [54] analysis of Clark's theory of the distribution of income between labour and aggregate capital (cf. p. 34, below).

The aggregation of physical units of productive equipments raises difficulties so that such analyses usually relate output in money terms (or value-added) to labour in units of labour-time, and capital in money value. Cobb and Douglas, following Moore, eventually demonstrated that a relation of the form $Q = AL^a K^{1-a}$ approximated closely to the national income accounts data of the share of labour and capital in G.N.P. [15]. This seemed to confirm the function as well as Clark's marginal productivity theory which it was derived to test (we shall not describe this derivation, cf. [36 pp. 31–44], nor the possible reasons for the statistical success. Fisher [18, 19] has suggested that the fit will be good for any production technology as long as the shares of capital and labour are constant over time, which was the case for the periods investigated; Shaikh [70] suggests that the function can be made to fit almost any random technology.) It is now accepted that the aggregate functions of this type are only rough characterisations of a theoretical position put forward by a number of economists in a number of ways.

But even as a theoretical concept the aggregate relation between output, labour and capital was not accepted as being free of logical flaws and inconsistencies. The passage of time

11

and the return to what seemed to be long-period analysis in Harrod's theory seemed to suggest, however, that the way was open to introduce this pre-Keynesian vestige of orthodox theory into the theoretical analysis of growth and dynamics. Further, it was argued by those who adopted this position, Keynes's theory applied only to the short period and had no application to a long-period situation. There was thus no other alternative to (nor anything illogical about) the readoption of the pre-Keynesian theory for the analysis of the problems of long-period capital accumulation that Harrod seemed to be posing.

Thus, taking Harrod's required capital coefficient, C_r, to be a simple capital–output ratio, K/Q, and introducing the production function relating Q to L and K, substitution of capital for labour under conditions of diminishing returns would make K/Q vary with the requirements for stable full employment growth. A variable ratio of K/L and thus K/Q could then be used to counter Harrod's concerns about the relations between the growth of the system and the level of employment over time. If too much capital were produced by the full-employment level of investment there would be no problem of excess capacity and dimmed expectations, the ratio of K/L would simply rise and more capital would be employed with each labourer. With labour scarce relative to capital the real wage would rise and the return to capital would fall, ensuring maintenance of full employment. There could never be a problem of insufficient investment or excess capacity for substitution of capital and labour (the change in K/L) and the corresponding adjustment in the wage and rate of interest would always assure full employment. Harrod's major concern was thus brushed back into the depths of the orthodox pre-1936 analysis, and was considered by many economists to be an illusory problem in long-period analysis (or, that since Keynes's theory showed how full employment could be attained one could safely assume that it could be maintained by proper Keynesian measures and thus taken as assumed for the analysis of the long period, but this is just what Harrod was trying to show could *not* be assumed). The same theory that Keynes – faced with the obvious unemployment of the slump – tried to dislodge was thus reinstated within the context of growth in the long run. It is hardly necessary to point out that this approach required the specification of capital and output in both physical and value terms (or a direct link between the two) that Keynes had considered impossible and rejected as being of little precise meaning.

Thus, while Keynes's theory rejected the use of the concept of aggregate capital and made little direct analysis of value and distribution (although the problems were discussed they were perhaps more clearly apparent in [47] and in the closely related work of Kalecki [46]) the orthodox teaching on these subjects persisted, the debate on their validity deflected by concern over the problems of employment. When Keynes's pupils and followers turned their minds to the broader theoretical problems of distribution within the context of an expanding system (which Harrod had purposely avoided) they found that the orthodox theory, along with the empirical studies as justification, still dominated academic opinion and teaching.

The anomaly of this situation was noted by Joan Robinson in a long essay on 'The Generalisation of the General Theory' [59], and in an article [60] that is commonly accepted as the starting point of the current debates (cf. Harcourt's description [29 pp. 11–12]). The challenge that she made was quite simply to define what is meant by the quantity of aggregate capital used in the production function. This, it should be stressed, was before the first introduction of such a function in an extension of a Harrod model of economic dynamics. The debate was then extended to the whole question of the use of a production function in a model of growth and the determinants of the growth process. (The previous debates, as we shall see below, were almost always carried out in static conditions or in the context of the stationary state, so that in this sense one could say that progress has been made over the earlier discussions.)

There was little active interest in the challenge to the production function (but cf. [11, 72]) until the publication in 1960 of Sraffa's *Production of Commodities* [78], which shows that there is no possible value aggregate of capital that can be defined independently of the rate of profits (or interest). Sraffa further suggested that, from the point of view of an industry producing a single product, the substitution of capital for labour that was assumed to result from a lower rate of interest could indeed just

13

as easily be accompanied by a higher rate of interest which contradicts the result implied by the orthodox analysis of prices and substitution.

A result similar to Sraffa's had been developed for the economy as a whole by Joan Robinson in [61], but was considered a 'curiosum' (as was a similar proposition made by Champernowne [11] who dismissed the case as 'unlikely'). Orthodox economists, however, felt that although Sraffa's result might be valid for one firm or industry, it could not be true for the economy as a whole and Levhari [52] tried to prove just that. His proof, however, was wrong as no less than four subsequent papers [56] showed. Sraffa's results had to be considered as generally valid for both the case of a single industry and the economy as a whole.

The more recent history of the debates has been in two directions (cf. [32]): first, a search for those conditions under which the relations developed by Sraffa cannot exist [7, 10, 74, 83], second, a steady change of position on what the orthodox (or neoclassical) theory 'really was' [82, 83], and most recently another attempt to disprove the validity of Sraffa's analysis [22] (the results of which are disproved in [51]).

Because of this confusing situation, the next chapter outlines the positions of a few well-known writers on capital theory in an attempt to see how the general argument developed into what was thought, in the early 1950s, to be a unified and coherent position on capital and its rate of return. This general position is based on the application of pricing or of supply and demand analysis to capital. The following relations have thus become associated with the orthodox theory (cf. [29 p. 122]):

(1) an association between lower rates of profits and higher values of capital per man employed;

(2) an association between lower rates of profits and higher capital–output ratios;

(3) an association between lower rates of profits and (through investment in more mechanised or 'round-about' methods of production) higher sustainable steady states of consumption per head (to a maximum); and

(4) that, in competitive conditions, the distribution of income between profit-receivers and wage-earners can be explained by a knowledge of marginal products and factor supplies.

14

All four propositions, it can be seen, require a quantity measure of capital that is independent of the rate of profits (or price of capital).

In the next chapter we will be interested to find out to what extent these ideas can be traced to previous writers before looking, in Chapter 3, at the arguments that have been produced in recent times to prove or disprove the four propositions.

2 Historical Background

Hicks has commented that capital is like a building, and 'though it is the same building, it looks quite different from different angles' [38 p. v]. As a direct example, consider the question: 'What is your capital?' You might say, 'my bank account', or 'my house', or 'my factory', or even 'all the goods and services that I possess, including myself, which yield me useful services'. Now if you were also asked: 'How much capital do you have?', the corresponding responses might be: '£100·89', or 'the amount I'd get from selling my house', or 'the cost of the factory' (or 'the present value of the discounted future profits expected from operating the factory') and finally, 'the discounted value of the expected future services of my possessions'.

Although very different, these responses show two things in common: first that capital has both a physical and a monetary aspect, and second, that there is a time dimension involved in values derived from expectations and discounting, which implies a direct relation to interest or profit rates. This latter aspect brings up the problems of value and distribution theory. Looked at in the broader context there can be no separate branch of theory treating capital independent of the approach to value, distribution and the determination of prices. In fact, many differences in approach to capital come from the emphasis on one of these aspects to the neglect of the others within a broader framework.

One problem, however, seems commonly accepted amongst writers on the subject. Think of the process of exchange in its simplest form, either in barter or money terms. I exchange, say, one bushel of corn (or £1) for a bushel of apples. I lose the corn and get the apples in return. After I have consumed the apples I am left with nothing to show for my corn except the memory of the eaten apples. If, on the other hand, I use my corn to buy, say, a printing press, and I use the printing press to do job-printing for others I will also be using up the machine as I had eaten the apples. But in the case of the machine it is considered normal that I should charge a price for printing work that covers not only my input costs, but also provides a fund for depreciation so that when the machine wears out I have enough money to buy another one. Then, in addition to this I also get a profit over and above the materials and running costs. When the apples were consumed I was left with nothing but memories, when my printing press wears out I have not only memories but profits *and* enough to replace the machine. Why do apples disappear but machines become a perpetual source of profit? If the apple–corn exchange is viewed as equitable then the corn–printing press exchange must appear inequitable for I appear to be paying too little for the machine since it gives me more gross return than its costs.

This problem can be seen in very early times in the Scholastics' debates over the justice of the payment of interest. Looking on exchange from the point of view of equal exchange and the 'just price' they believed that the use of a good should be equal to its price. Interest could not be claimed on goods which had to be destroyed to be used – to borrow apples meant to want to eat apples and one could not claim anything in addition as interest. But for goods that could be used without destroying their usefulness, interest could be justified, as, for example, in the case of a house which could provide housing services indefinitely as long as it was retained in good repair. Thus interest could be justifiably demanded on such a *non-fungible* good, the payment taking the form of the return of the house plus the payment for the use of the house, which would exceed the just price of the house itself. (On this argument it is obvious that the Thomists should have argued against interest on money loans for the use of money was obviously for spending, i.e. it was destroyed in use and thus *fungible*. Interest would have been unjust for it would demand not only the money back but also a payment for its use when indeed they were one and the same thing.)

For the Physiocrats the distinction was between agricultural and other production. On the planting of one seed I can expect to reap many more. On this relation was built the concept of the *produit net*, or net surplus that arose not out of economic exchange which they also held to be equitable (but in physical terms) but from the fertility of the soil which was claimed as the natural right of the nobles.

Smith extended the concept of net productivity to all production, distinguishing between different states of society characterised by different rules of exchange. When 'accumulation of stock and appropriation of land' has taken place profits are attributed to the accumulators of stock for it is only in this way that the division of labour can take place.

For Marx, the problem was posed in terms of equal exchange as well – if products were just sold for the value represented by the simple labour time necessary to produce them, then there could be no additional mark-up for profit added to their costs of production or their selling prices. Capital is then seen as a set of social relations where private ownership of capital forces labour-power to the equivalent of any other commodity freely bought and sold. But unlike other commodities which sell at their value, labour can also produce value. Capital is that set of social relations where the capitalists can determine the conditions of working and especially the length of the working day such that labour produces more value in a working day than its own value, i.e. surplus value. The existence of surplus value under conditions of equal exchange is the basis of capitalists' profit that results from the social relations of production found under capitalism.

In more recent times Wicksell has cited that 'paradoxical phenomenon' whereby 'goods which exhaust or seem to exhaust their whole content of usefulness' can continue as a 'perpetuum mobile' with their 'entire value remain[ing] stored up for the owner' which always 'provides him with an income'.

This paradox, says Wicksell, is 'the real pith of the theory of capital' [86 p. 99]. This echoes the problem as posed by Böhm-Bawerk, 'What we have to explain is the fact that, when capital is productively employed, there regularly remains over in the hands of the undertaker a surplus proportional to the amount of his capital. . . . Why is there this constant surplus value?' [5 pp. 77–8].

Schumpeter [68 ch. V] also takes the same line of attack in putting forward his own explanation of this unaccounted income. He argues that in equilibrium under competitive conditions, capital should be produced until its earnings just repay its costs of production, that any excess should be eliminated by the claims of the original factors that produce capital, namely labour and land.

Thus, what was a justification for interest to the Scholastics and a fact of natural economic organisation for the Physiocrats, becomes the basic conundrum of modern-day theorists and the basis for the study of capital and the return to capital.

While the problem at issue is more or less commonly accepted by nineteenth-century writers, the approach and especially the terminology is less uniform. Thus, just as capital can be viewed in a physical or financial form, the return – the unexplained excess – to capital is called either interest or profit. But the terms are not consistently used in this sense. In the neoclassical theory, for example, a sharp distinction is made between the productive inputs and physical forms as well as between the owners and the users of these inputs. Thus, the entrepreneur (or, in English, undertaker or enterpriser) is the organiser of production, hiring labour services and capital services to combine to produce output. For the capital services he can either hire the services or borrow money which he then uses to buy a machine to provide himself with the required services. The income from the productive employment of factors is then wages for labour services, interest to be paid on the borrowed money capital, which leaves profit as the return to the organiser of production. Profit in competitive equilibrium is then zero for the organiser adds no productive service in addition to any labour he might directly provide which would be considered as wages. Interest is thus the return to the money capital that has been provided by the capitalist, but operated in the form of a machine by the entrepreneur in producing goods. Interest thus may be seen as a part of the total output attributed to the physical equipment and paid to the capitalist because he provided the money loan that allowed the physical capital to be purchased.

Such a classificatory scheme keeps a separation between interest and profit, but not between money and physical capital. The Classical economists looked at the matter from the point of view of the early industrial revolution and assumed that the capitalist and the entrepreneur were identical and received a profit on the employment of his capital. Interest was reserved for the return to money loans. In the current debates it is accepted procedure to drop the entrepreneur out of the analysis (partly because the models all assume either stationary or steady-state equilibrium so that the return to the entrepreneurial function would be zero) and to accept Keynes's distinction that the return to productive equipment be called profit so that interest refers solely to money loans, however used. Again, since most of the analysis is in equilibrium terms with perfect foresight money has little role and can be left out of the analysis along with borrowing and lending. One is thus left with simply the return to capital which is consistently called *profit* by the followers of the Classical tradition and *interest* by the neoclassical adherents. Under the equilibrium, steady-state assumptions they both come to the same thing (throughout Chapter 3 we shall use profits rather than interest to represent the returns to capital in the sense of means of production of output).

The previous discussion has focused on one aspect of the problem, the return to capital and the definition of capital. But this ignores a prior question concerning the accumulation of capital. We do well to keep in mind that these are interrelated questions, for the accumulation of capital implies the production of output in excess of the productive inputs and the apportionment of this net output among the participating inputs and the use to which they put their share of the net output. To the extent that capital's return can be identified with the 'unaccountable' surplus the further accumulation of capital is dependent on the existence of and the use made of the return to capital. Many writers attempt logically to separate the two problems by the assumption of a stationary state where accumulation is zero by definition, leaving only the cause and the size of the return to the existing and unchanging amount of capital to be determined. With these provisos in mind we start our investigation into the development of approaches to capital theory.

ADAM SMITH

Smith was primarily interested in the problem of economic development and capital accumulation. The role of the division of labour in this process is well known. The welfare of the nation is governed by two principles: the degree of the division of labour and the proportion of productive to non-productive labour, Smith giving greater weight to the former aspect.

The capitalist and his accumulated stock is one of the main regulators, along with the extent of the market, of the degree to which the division of labour can be carried for 'the accumulation of stock must, in the nature of things, be previous to the division of labour, so labour can be more and more subdivided in proportion only as stock is previously more and more accumulated' [71 p. 119], since, 'the accumulation of stock is previously necessary for carrying on this great improvement in the productive powers of labour, so that accumulation naturally leads to this improvement'.

Stock can be distinguished from other goods by the fact that it 'puts industry in motion', all other goods being consumption goods. 'In order to put industry in motion, three things are requisite: materials to work upon, tools to work with, and the wages or recompense for the sake of which work is done' [71 p. 128]. This stock can be divided into fixed capital which will 'increase the productive powers of labour, or enable the same number of labourers to perform a much greater quantity of work' [71 p. 124], and circulating capital 'which furnishes the materials and wages of labour and puts industry into motion' [71 p. 126]. The remaining part of the nation's stocks being 'that portion which is reserved for immediate consumption, and of which the characteristic is, that it affords no revenue or profit' [71 p. 121].

The distinction between fixed and circulating capital, it should be noted, is not one of time-dimension or durability, but whether 'it affords a revenue or profit' with 'or without circulating or changing masters' [71 p. 121]. The two are interconnected in that 'every fixed capital is both originally derived from, and requires to be continually supported by a circulating capital' for 'no fixed capital can yield any revenue but by means of circulating capital' [71 p. 122]. 'Different occupations require very different proportions between the fixed and circulating capitals employed in them' [71 p. 120]. To note the distinction between fixed and circulating capital one has merely to look at the example of seed corn which Smith says, 'is properly a fixed capital' for 'though it goes backwards and forwards between the ground and the granary, it never changes masters, and therefore does not properly circulate' [71 p. 121]. It is obvious that Smith's definition is different from that commonly employed today.

That stock will be used to put industry in motion when it is sufficient to satisfy 'immediate needs' is obvious to Smith for 'everyman of common understanding will endeavour to employ whatever stock he can command in procuring either present enjoyment or future profit' [71 p. 123].

As to why profit can be earned Smith is not explicit, but the employment of stock as capital 'is always repaid with great profit, and increases the annual produce by a much greater value than that of the support which such improvements require' [71 p. 124]. Whatever part of his stock a man employs as a capital, 'he always expects it to be replaced to him with a profit' [71 p. 147] as long as it is used to employ productive labour.

For Smith profit on capital is evidently connected very closely with the increase in output that it brings about. Each new employment of stock is seen as increasing the productivity of labour by increasing the division of labour, and it is from this increase that the capitalist claims his profit, for

> The annual produce of the land and labour of any nation can be increased in its value by no other means but by increasing either the number of its productive labourers, or the productive powers of those labourers who had before been employed. The number of its productive labourers, it is evident can never be much increased, but in consequence of an increase of capital, or of the funds destined to maintaining them.

The productive powers can be affected 'in consequence either of some addition and improvement to those machines and instruments which facilitate and abridge labour, or of a more proper division and distribution of employments' [71 p. 152]. There seems little question that profit is primarily a result of the increased productivity resulting from the increased employment of stock as capital.

The profit that can be derived from continually increasing

22

the employment of stock must 'necessarily diminish' as 'It becomes gradually more and more difficult to find within a country a profitable *method* of employing any new capital' [71 p. 157]. Thus, as the possibilities for increasing productivity become fewer in number, and the only alternative is to increase stock employed in existing methods of division of labour, 'there arises, in consequence, a competition between different capitals' for markets, and for labour, acting to push down the price of output and increase the wage of labour which 'sinks the profits of stock'. This in turn reacts on the loan market where 'the price that can be paid for the use of it [stock] that is, the rate of interest, must necessarily be diminished' [71 p. 157]. Thus, it is not clearly possible to say whether Smith thought profits on stock were permanent, or that profits were a natural element in the determination of price. It seems clear enough, however, that Smith did not regard profit as resulting from anything inherent in the capital goods themselves, but from the changes in the division of labour (the method of production) that increasing stock made possible. When these further possibilities are exhausted profits fall towards zero, and Smith would have expected that in a stationary state profits would be 'very low' [71 p. 43] if not zero. This, of course, explains why Smith did not believe that capitalists, as receivers of profit, were well served by continued growth (nor that they were the cause of the productivity of changes in the division of labour for the division is not caused by the mere accumulation of stock, nor is it due to the innovation of the capitalists, but to 'the invention of the common workmen' [71 p. 5]). One could even argue that in the stationary equilibrium of the Classical system profits would not exist, thus making Smith an early forerunner of modern-day concerns over the relation between the surplus product and capital equipment.

RICARDO

Ricardo follows Smith in the treatment of capital as a fund for the employment of labour: 'Capital is that part of the wealth of a country which is employed in production, and consists of food, clothing, tools, raw materials, machinery, &c. necessary to give effect to labour' [58 p. 95]. This is about the only point of similarity, however, for Ricardo takes conditions of durability as the distinguishing feature of fixed versus circulating capital and rejects Smith's explanation of the effect of accumulation on profit, maintaining that 'no accumulation of capital will permanently lower profits, unless there be some permanent cause for the rise of wages' [58 p. 289]. However, 'The natural tendency of profits then is to fall; for, in the progress of society and wealth, the additional quantity of food required is obtained by the sacrifice of more and more labour' [58 p. 120].

The existence of profit, in Ricardo's theory, depends on the existence of a surplus over wage-costs on marginal or no-rent land. Thus, accumulation and growth of population cause the difference between wages and output to fall as less productive land is brought into use (or as land is used more intensively). With wages determined by social and physiological factors the difference between the wage and production on marginal land emerges as a residual which can fall to some 'very low' level which will 'arrest all accumulation' [58 p. 120]. The only possible exception to this result is in 'improvements in machinery, connected with the production of necessaries', 'discoveries in the science of agriculture', and through trade for necessaries [58 p. 120]. Thus, although the general results are the same as Smith's the mechanism is quite different, especially with differing methods of production not accounting for profits but acting as a palliative to keep them from falling.

As Ricardo thought that labour proved in general terms to be a good measure of value it followed that labour could serve as a measure for the accumulation of stock. It is in the relation of labour embodied to value and price that Ricardo takes the most concern over capital; in its distinction as between fixed and circulating and in terms of the time period of production.

> It appears then that the division of capital into different proportions of fixed and circulating capital, employed in different trades, introduces a considerable modification to the rule, which is of universal application when labour is almost exclusively employed in production; namely, that commodities never vary in value, unless a greater or less quantity of labour be bestowed on their production [58 p. 38]

24

and 'It is hardly necessary to say, that commodities which have the same quantity of labour bestowed on their production, will differ in exchangeable value, if they cannot be brought to market in the same time' [58 p. 37]. This concern over the relation of periods of production ([16] emphasises the 'Austrian' character of Ricardo's theory) and proportions of different types of capital in different industries is bound up with Ricardo's search for an invariable measure of value (cf. [78] for a solution to the problem) and indicate that he was dissatisfied with labour as a *measure* of value (which in turn indicates that Ricardo would have had hesitations about the measurement of the stock of goods incorporated in the national capital, either in terms of embodied or accumulated labour). Ricardo's emphasis on labour and time periods is, however, to have a strong influence on the further development of capital theory as found in the Austrian approach (cf. [23]) and current orthodoxy (cf. [26]).

JEVONS

While accusing Ricardo of putting economic science on the wrong track, Jevons was willing to follow two basic features of Ricardo's analysis. This was primarily because Jevons thought that the effects of capital and capital accumulation were independent of exchange relations *per se*.

Capital has two main aspects in Jevons's view: 'Capital is concerned with time' and 'allows us to expend labour in advance' [43 pp. 226–7] and as such 'consists merely in the aggregate of those commodities which are required for sustaining labourers of any kind or class engaged in work' [43 p. 226]. (This passage points up a basic difference from Smith who would have insisted that the modifier 'productive' be prefixed to labourers; likewise, what Jevons would include in a physical enumeration of capital would be enlarged to this extent: rented houses, etc. – cf. [43 p. 270 and p. 251 n.].)

Thus, it is not so much technical productivity (or the division of labour) but the amount of time that capital allows for the lengthening of production –

I would say, then, in the most general manner, that what-ever improvements in the supply of commodities lengthen the average interval between the moment when labour is exerted and its ultimate result or purpose accomplished, such improvements depend upon the use of capital. Whenever we overlook the irrelevant complication introduced by the division of labour and the frequency of exchange, all employments of capital resolve themselves into the fact of time elapsing between the beginning and the end of industry [43 p. 229].

This approach implies that capital has at least a twol dimensional concept – physical and temporal. To highlighthis, Jevons distinguishes between the 'amount of capitat invested' and the 'amount of investment of capital' [43 p. 229]; it is the second that takes into account the time dimension, 'the length of time [capital] remains invested'. Since investment represents the maintenance of labour in production, capital invested is to be measured in terms of days' labour. Two processes of production, each requiring twenty days' labour, but one twice as long as the other, will require the same absolute amount of capital invested (maintenance of labour for twenty days) but the second has double the investment of capital for the labour is invested for twice as long before the end of the process. On the other side of production, the use of produced goods represents disinvestment so that Jevons's overall view of capital is that of accumulating labour employed over the period of production and a decumulation of this labour as the output of the process is consumed (or used to produce saleable or consumable output). The simple sum of all labour-days will thus exceed the actual labour embodied. To solve this problem Jevons introduces an 'average time of investment' which, 'provided capital be invested and uninvested continuously and in simple proportion to time . . . the amount of investment will be in every case the greatest amount of capital multiplied by half the time elapsing from the beginning to the end of investment' [43 p. 231]. (This assumes that simple interest is paid and that all periods' inputs and outputs are the same, cf. Wicksell's assumption of a 'constant taking up' of capital. Jevons does make the point that compound interest is the relevant case and takes examples, but assumes that the general results will be the same whether interest is simple or compound.)

The return to capital is thus determined by the increase in output occasioned by the increased length of the process of production or 'provided that we may suppose the produce for the same amount of labour to vary as some continuous function of the time elapsing between the expenditure of labour and the enjoyment of results' [43 p. 240], but that after a certain point it will not be possible to keep on 'increasing produce from the greater application of capital' [43 p. 241].

Thus, as each increase in time elapsed in production increases the capital invested, the increase in produce will increase but at a declining rate and thus, 'the rate of increase of the produce divided by the whole produce' will fall towards zero [43 p. 241], i.e. 'the rate of interest varies inversely as the time of investment'. Since capital invested varies directly with time it also varies inversely with the rate of interest. Thus, 'unless there be constant progress in the arts, the rate (of interest) must tend to sink towards zero, supposing accumulation of capital to go on' [43 p. 245]. The rate of profits thus varies as in Smith, with diminishing returns to the length of the period of production replacing diminishing returns to the division of labour; which is in contrast to Ricardo, for the rate of profits is independent of the rate of wages which is 'determined by the increment of produce which it enables the labourer to obtain' [43 p. 246].

For Jevons it seemed obvious that capital was a subsistence fund for the employment of labour and that only when advanced to labour as wages was capital able to put labour to work long before the produce became available. Thus, irrespective of its physical make-up Jevons considered capital as embodied wages or labour time, for 'labour is the starting-point in production' [43 p. 255]. But this view of capital or 'free' capital ('the wages of labour, either in its transitory form of money, or its real form of food and other necessities of life') will not in general be of the same magnitude in its 'real' and 'transitory' forms, for to turn a physical set of goods into money value (or a sum of money into a set of physical goods) requires the specification of wage rates and relative prices, and, to the extent that the rate of interest enters the determination of relative prices and wages, the rate of interest itself must be known.

27

But it is precisely this that the process is supposed to determine (cf. [79]).

Jevons is not clear whether interest is a result of abstinence or the higher productivity resulting from lengthening the production process (he seems to place more emphasis on the latter, although Böhm-Bawerk [6], who borrows heavily from Jevons's approach, classified him as an eclectic genius who could not quite make up his mind). None the less, his concept of an average period of investment of capital was a major influence on the Austrian approach to the problem of capital. It seems clear that Jevons is closer to Smith than Ricardo in approach and result, although his view of capital as labour accumulated over time is close to Ricardo. In this sense capital cannot be considered as a factor of production distinct from land and labour in Jevons's scheme.

THE AUSTRIAN SCHOOL – BÖHM-BAWERK

The general approach to economic phenomena based on final consumption and individual utility was put forward by Menger at about the same time as Jevons, but without the mathematical embellishments. A basic distinguishing feature of the Austrian approach is the ordering of goods in terms of their stage in the production process, from original inputs to final outputs. Consumption goods are called goods of the first order and higher than first-order goods are those which serve as inputs (intermediate goods) for the production of goods of a lower order. Thus all goods save those of the highest order (original goods) are produced goods used in the production of goods of a lower order, until final, or first-order, goods are consumed.

The valuation of goods then works by a chain process or process of reduction, starting with the valuation of goods of the first order made by consumers in their purchases of final goods. The values of the goods of the first order then determine the value of the higher order goods that have been used as inputs and so on as value is imputed to all goods from first order to highest order, or to the original factors of production. Böhm-Bawerk's role in the Austrian theory was to combine the Ricardian approach to capital in terms of labour and time with the 'new' marginal approach to pricing through utility.

Dealing with capital from the point of view of the rank or hierarchy of goods it is obvious that capital cannot be conceived of as an original or independent factor of production (good of the highest order) for only land (or more broadly, natural resources) and labour are naturally occurring goods and thus fit the definition of goods of the highest order in that they are not themselves produced but enter into the production of other goods. As capital goods are produced goods under this view they are no different from any other intermediate or middle goods and the problem of capital and its return becomes, 'in the last resort', simply 'a problem of value' [5 p. 425]. Capital is thus associated with the distance or the number of stages of intermediate goods that are required between the highest and lowest order goods. The degree of this intermediation is the basis of what the Austrians called the 'period of production', or the 'roundaboutness' of production.

> All consumption goods which man produces come into existence through a co-operation of human power with natural powers, which latter are partly economic, partly free. By means of these primary productive powers man may make the consumption goods he desires, either immediately, or through the medium of intermediate products called Capital. The latter method demands a sacrifice of time, but it has an advantage in the quantity of product, and this advantage although perhaps in decreasing ratio, is associated with every prolongation of the roundabout way of production [6 p. 91].

There are thus, in the Austrian view, two 'original productive powers', labour power and the powers of nature. Capital is not a thing, but a way of temporally and physically combining labour and natural resources to produce intermediate goods which are not used for consumption, but whose production allows a greater production of consumption goods per unit of labour expended.

In order then to determine why capital should have a positive return Böhm-Bawerk poses two questions: 'How does capital originate?' and 'What is the nature of capital's productive work?' 'The first question has to do with the theory of the formation or accumulation of capital; the second, with the productive function of capital' [6 p. 75].

All human production aims at the obtaining of goods for consumption. These consumption goods are dependent for their existence on physical conditions, and are subject to natural laws. To obtain them ... we must seek to bring about such combinations of active forces as will result in the desired object. Thus we get a product which has come into existence under natural law and continues to exist under natural law. Now look a little more closely at the nature of the power which man can employ towards these productive combinations. It is made up of two components very dissimilar in amount – first, an enormous mass of powers which the natural world exerts spontaneously year out year in; and second, the much more limited natural powers which reside in the human organism [6 p. 78].

Now, as we have seen, the way in which we get command of these natural treasures is through the other branch of our productive endowment, our own personal powers. We put forth our labour in all kinds of wise combinations with natural processes. Thus all that we get in production is the result of two, and only two, elementary productive powers – Nature and Labour. This is one of the most certain ideas in the theory of production. Man finds ready to hand an abundance of natural processes, and allies her own powers with them. What nature by herself does, and what man does along with her – these form the double source from which all our goods come. .... There is no place for any third primary source. These two elements, then, *technically*, do everything in the work of production [6 pp. 79–80].

Thus, the Austrian position would imply that the more capitalistic the production process, the more stages (or ranks of intermediate goods) would exist between the original application of land and labour and the production of final (first-order) goods; and that this increase in the length of the process would be associated with a similar increase in the quantity of final goods available at the end of the process.

The adoption of capitalistic methods of production is followed by two consequences. . . . One is an advantage, the other a disadvantage. The advantage . . . consists in the greater technical productiveness of those methods. . . . The disadvantage connected with the capitalist method of production is its sacrifice of time. The roundabout ways of capital are fruitful but long; they procure us more or better consumption goods, but only at a later period of time. This proposition, no less than the former, is one of the ground pillars of the theory of capital [6 p. 82].

Here 'roundaboutness' takes the place of the division of labour in producing increasing output, but, as in Jevons, there are diminishing returns to increases in the roundaboutness of a process. The degree of capitalisation or roundaboutness of a process (again echoing Jevons) is thus, 'the period of time which elapses *on the average* between the expenditure of the original productive powers, labour and uses of land, as successively employed in any work, and the turning out of the finished consumption goods. Production is more or less capitalistic according to the average remoteness of the period at which the productive powers exerted during the process are paid' [6 pp. 88–9].

As an example, let A and B be two processes of production employing the same amount of labour, 100 man-days, and proceeding for the same absolute time period, ten years. The concept of the average period is to attempt to distinguish between these two processes which are identical from the absolute amounts of time and labour input, i.e. to take into account the time distribution of the use of productive powers (see Table 1).

Table 1

	$t-10$	$t-9$	$t-8$	$t-7$	$t-6$	$t-5$	$t-4$	$t-3$	$t-2$	$t-1$	t	Total
A	1	1	1	1	1	1	1	1	1	1	90	100
B	20	20	5	5	5	5	5	5	5	5	20	100

Thus A requires one man-year of labour in each of the ten years before final production, and 90 units just as the product comes to final fruition (the 90 units are thus not invested for any 'time'). To derive the average amount of time that labour is invested we follow the formula

$$T = \frac{L_1 + 2L_2 + 3L_3 + NL_n}{L_1 + L_2 + L_3 + L_n}.$$

The numerators for A and B are then respectively $A = 10 + 9 + 8 + 7 + 6 + 5 + 4 + 3 + 2 + 1 + (90 \times 0) = 55$, $B = 200 + 180 + 40 + 35 + 30 + 25 + 20 + 15 + 10 + (20 \times 0) = 560$, so that dividing each by 100 gives $A_t = 0.55$ and $B_t = 5.6$. Thus the average production period for B is roughly ten times as great as for A and it can be said to be ten times more capitalistic (and should produce slightly less than ten times as much output). (Note also that we say, more capitalistic, not that it employs more capital.)

Like Jevons (and Wicksell) Böhm-Bawerk notes that 'It is only in methods of production where the expenditure of original powers is distributed equally over the whole production period that the absolute length of the process affords at the same time the proper measure for the degree of capitalism' [6 p. 90].

Although Böhm-Bawerk emphasises the time distribution of the application of the two productive powers (as a simple average) he also looks on the existing stock of goods of intermediate order as the fund that gives employment of labour and also, like Jevons, on the embodied resources in these assembled intermediate goods. Just like Jevons, he thus relies on a valuation of these heterogeneous goods in money terms as well as in terms of the simple average period.

The explanation of the existence of profit is, however, more subtle. First, in agreement with Smith, accumulation is a necessary pre-condition of the application of more roundabout methods. Thus, at any point in time there will be in existence finished goods just emerging from production, and a range of other goods in intermediate stages (or 'future' goods). For the Austrians the existence of profit is to be found, not in the famous three factors (difference in provision and want, underestimation of the future, and technical superiority of present goods) but in the simple fact that labour has no accumulated wealth and thus must accept less than the full value of what it produces because it cannot wait until the end of lengthy processes.

Thus, they suppose that the utility of a finished good now is greater than the utility of a future (unfinished) good now. But 'The labourers urgently need present goods, and cannot, or can scarcely turn their own labour to any account; they will, therefore, to a man rather sell their labour cheaply than not sell it at all' [6 p. 385]. In fact, what they do is to exchange their future goods for present goods at equal utility value. But since a future good has a lower utility than a finished good a greater quantity of future goods must be exchanged against present goods to make the exchange one of equality of utility. The profit of the capitalist thus results from his holding this additional quantity of future goods until they become finished goods. Thus there is still equal exchange (one should note similarities with Marx's explanation of surplus value), no exploitation, but the difference in utility that accompanies the 'technical superiority' of present goods (later to become time preference) and the unequal wealth positions of labourers and capitalists explains the existence of profit on capital, despite the insistence that there is no such thing in the sense of adding to production.

The actual movement of the rate of interest (profit) will also follow previous writers' beliefs and be temporally downward, but will depend on

three elements or factors which act as decisive determinants of the rate of interest: the Amount of the national subsistence fund, the Number of workers provided for by it, and the Degree of productivity in extending production periods. . . . In a community interest will be high in proportion as the national subsistence fund is low, as the number of labourers employed by the same is great, and as the surplus returns connected with any further extension of the production period continue high. Conversely, interest will be low the greater the subsistence fund, the fewer the labourers, and the quicker the fall of the surplus returns [6 p. 401].

Thus, a relative surplus of capital will tend to drive down the rate of interest, as will a scarcity of labour relative to capital and the onset of diminishing returns. The continued accumulation of capital relative to the growth of labour should then tend to produce Smith's result of a falling interest rate until a position of stationary state is reached.

33

J. B. CLARK

Clark emphasised a different aspect of the relation between capital and time as well as taking his insights from a different area of Ricardian theory. Clark first of all distinguishes between concrete physical capital-goods and capital as a fund of goods or a sum of money: 'Capital-goods imply waiting for the fruits of labor. Capital, on the contrary, implies the direct opposite of this: it is the means of avoiding all waiting. It is solidified time, or the material result of waiting on a vast scale' [12 p. 311].

But here Clark departs markedly from the Austrians for he identifies this solid 'thing' capital as a distinct factor of production. The physical aspect of capital thus highlights the fixity of capital at any point in time and suggests to Clark the possibility that its return can be treated just like any other fixed factor, for example land (only with capital the fixity depends on the time period chosen, with land it does not).

> Tools are productive, but time is the condition of getting tools – this is the simple and literal fact. The round-about or time-consuming mode of using labor insures efficient capital-goods. Granting that time be used for this purpose, we may say that 'time is productive'; but we must be careful to keep in view the fact that it is the tools secured by time that do the producing [12 p. 309].

Thus having paid lip-service to the importance of time, Clark attributes the productivity of long processes not to time but to the goods themselves. Since the tools cannot be anything but fixed at any point of time Clark sets out to develop a general theoretical system by applying Ricardo's theory of rent to capital and labour to determine the distribution of income as well as the dynamic path of economic development.

To carry out such a task capital had to be considered as a unique quantity that could, as the theory required, be held constant as labour varied, and become a variable when labour was the fixed factor. To satisfy this requirement Clark emphasised the fact that over long periods of time physical capital was being used, wearing out and being replaced by other physical capital-goods that were not the exact replicas of those they replaced. Thus although capital in some abstract sense continued to exist (and expand) throughout time, its actual concrete physical composition was ever-changing.

The most distinctive single fact about what we have termed capital is the fact of permanence. It lasts; and it must last, if industry is to be successful. . . . Yet you must destroy *capital-goods* in order not to fail. . . . Capital-goods, then, not only *may* go to destruction, but *must* be destroyed, if industry is to be successful; and they must do so in order that capital may last. . . . It is this idea of permanence that originally gave a name to the kind of wealth that is of such capital, or vital, importance that it must always be kept intact [12 p. 117].

The fact that capital must remain intact and constant while at the same time it must be used up in production over time and replaced, Clark calls the transmigration of capital or the transmutation of physical capitals into different forms despite the fact that capital stays unchanged (or simply what Marx called the process of realisation of capital).

With this distinction of definition *capital*, although permanent, is mobile and can be shifted from use to use, while *capital-goods*, the temporal form of capital, are perishable and fixed. Thus, says Clark, at any point in time capital is fixed in amount and shape, just like land. Its return can then be analysed in the same manner. 'Rent is the aggregate of the lump sums earned by capital goods; while interest is the fraction of itself that is earned by the permanent fund of capital' [12 p. 124].

Interest is not a fraction of buildings, ships, horses, etc.: it is a fraction of the permanent fund that an endless series of such shifting things embodies. With rent, on the contrary, it is the concrete forms that come into prominence. Every instrument that helps to constitute the permanent fund of capital earns, during its active existence, a certain definite quantity of wealth, which can be measured in a lump sum. The axe may earn two dollars; the spade, four dollars; the boat, fifty dollars; the building, a hundred thousand dollars, etc. In all these things there is no idea of a percentage connected with these earnings. We can, however, reduce that part of the gross product of an instrument which is really a net income to a percentage of the value of the instrument. If we do this, we shall have reduced the rent, with a certain deduction, to the form of interest [12 p. 335].

'Net rent is, then, nothing more than interest regarded from another point of view: it is an aggregate of lump sums, each of which represents the net earnings of some instrument. It is identical in amount with interest, and it becomes interest the moment that we reduce it to a fraction of the value of the instruments that earn it' [12 p. 337]. There is then a unique relation, at any point in time, between the value of capital goods and the physical representations of that permanent fund of capital used in actual production.

In Ricardo's theory rent was determined by the productivity of the marginal land in relation to intramarginal units, the total product left after the deduction of rent being the return to wages and profits combined. All these returns would be changing as the system accumulated capital, brought less productive land under cultivation (or used existing land more intensively) and thus evolved towards the stationary state where rent, wages and profits would be constant (save technical advance and trade). Here the only equilibrium is the stationary state.

Clark, however, rejects this approach and introduces the concept of a static and dynamic system. He defines a dynamic system as one that is characterised by the following: (a) population increasing; (b) capital increasing; (c) methods of production improving; (d) forms of industrial establishment improving; and (e) the wants of consumers multiplying [12 p. 56]. Thus, when all these characteristics of an actual system are assumed to be *absent*, the system is said to be *static*. For Clark this static state is 'an imaginary state', which 'reveals facts of real life', despite the fact that 'there is . . . no society that is thus static' [12 p. 60]. It is Clark's belief (and the basic assumption in all his work) that this imaginary state of affairs exhibits laws that 'continue to act in a dynamic one'. 'We are, then, studying the realities of the modern progressive state when we examine the characteristics of the imaginary static one' [12 p. 60].

In a static state, of course, capital-goods are given and must be defined to determine marginal products; it is on this assumption that one justifies the use of the theory of rent. But when Clark calculates the static final productivities in the imaginary static conditions the concrete physical capital-goods no longer have fixed physical form or shape: 'Where there is a capital of five hundred dollars for each worker, that fund is in one set of forms; and where there is a capital of a thousand dollars per man, it is in a different set' [12 p. 159]. 'That the relative *amounts* of labor and capital should change, means that the *forms* of both should change' [12 p. 160].

Thus the calculation of final productivity of labour, which requires holding capital constant, refers not to capital-goods at all, but to the money amount of capital for,

> As we take away laborers, we leave the capital everywhere unchanged in amount; but we change the forms of it in every one of the industries, so as to make it accurately fit the needs of the slightly reduced working force. . . . The abandoned pick and shovel become, by miracle of transmutation, an improvement in the quality of horse and cart. There are fewer men digging; but they have as much capital as ever, and they have it in a form in which, with their reduced numbers, they can use it [12 p. 170].

But it is clear that Clark is still in his imaginary state where everything is not only arbitrarily held constant, but where everything that is constant is arbitrarily changeable: 'How nearly unthinkable is that essential part of the test, the prompt transmuting of the capital into forms that the reduced working force would require!' [12 p. 71].

Clark's only justification for this approach of equilibrium by imagination is that transmutation actually occurs in dynamic situations – capital does indeed change its form over time to accommodate to the supply of labour and there must be some explanation for this movement. Clark believes that the dynamic movement is given by the static laws, that the imaginary static state gives the values of equilibrium towards which the dynamic state actually will be moving (he likens his static equilibrium values with factor rewards equal to final productivities as similar to the natural values of the Classics) [12 p. 400]. 'The forces of change, however, can never be understood without first having a knowledge of the forces of rest' and 'The static state which has been here pictured is the one toward which society is at every instant tending . . . [which] should then be thought of as an ideal arrangement . . . it is a shape and a mode of action that the real world carries within it' [12 pp. 402-3].

But even this result is only tentative for 'changes themselves and their effects are all subjects for economic dynamics. Static science recognises one natural standard of wages for one time; but static laws, pure and simple, as they work in an actual and dynamic society, never give the same rate at different dates, but rather an endless succession of static rates' [12 p. 409]. The dynamic system may thus be chasing an ever-changing moving static target (although Clark believed that the law of averages would cancel out many forces for change, thus leaving the target rather stable).

Clark left his study of true dynamics still to be written; all that was necessary was to believe that the imaginary static state exerted an influence over the dynamic development of the system. Accepting this assumption gave Clark a theory of economic causation; 'The science of rent is a science of economic causation, which traces products to their sources. The rent getter is the product creator' [12 p. 196]. From this point of view it is easy to show that capital is not only productive, but that it is 'deserving' of the profits that it earns.

The question is not so much that capital is productive for Clark agrees with the Classics that

The thing, then, that is ultimately essential for production is labor. But if time is to intervene between the labor and the enjoyment of its fruits, the work may be first spent on capital goods, which are a requisite of an accelerated rate of production. What they insure is an added quantity of product. They are not, however, a requisite of production *as a process*, for wealth may be created without them [12 p. 310].

But, at any arbitrarily defined point in time where the system is held in suspended animation their return will be determined by this productivity at an imaginary margin. To translate this rental into a rate of interest, as Clark admits, requires the capital value of the physical capital-goods, just as Jevons and Böhm-Bawerk before him.

Clark's most distinctive contribution is then not his application of the theory of rent to labour and capital as well as land (Wicksteed [88] developed the theory in even greater detail on the micro level) but the introduction of the static equilibrium as a purely imaginary construction, and the assumption that this construction was of use in economic analysis.

WICKSELL

Wicksell considered himself as primarily an expositor of the Austrian theory, although he was little convinced by the concept of an average period of production and eventually was led to abandon it as he continued to integrate the Austrian with other approaches. Wicksell was also one of the first economists to notice that there was an ambiguity in the application of the theory of rent to capital taken as a whole. He objected that while there were definable margins at which additional units of land or labour would fail to add to output enough to cover their own costs this would be true of capital only from the point of view of the employment of specific capital-goods [87 p. 198] and on the assumption of given wages and rents (cf. [86 p. 137]) for a single producer. It would not be generally true for capital taken as a whole. Thus, while final productivity could be determined for land and labour on an individual or aggregate basis, it could not be applied to national capital on an aggregate basis. 'If we consider an increase in the total capital of society, then it is by no means true that the consequent increase in the total social product would regulate the rate of interest' [87 p. 148].

The explanation of this curious divergence is quite simple. Whereas labour and land are measured each in terms of its own *technical* unit (e.g. working days or month; acre per annum) capital, on the other hand, as we have already shown, is reckoned, in common parlance, as a sum of *exchange value* – whether in money or as in average products. In other words, each particular capital good is measured by a unit extraneous to itself [87 p. 149].

Thus the approach in terms of productivity would have to be limited to particular types of capital-goods, each measured in terms of its own particular type of service (as Wicksteed [88] had insisted, e.g. steam power for a steam engine). But this would leave capital in general undefined and a rate of interest on capital indeterminate for want of a method of combining the different types of capital and the different types of services derived from them in production.

Even then we should only know the *yield* of the various objects at a particular moment, but nothing at all about the value of the goods themselves, which it is necessary to know to calculate the rate of interest, which in equilibrium is the same on all capital . . . it is futile to attempt . . . to derive the value of capital-goods from their own costs of production or reproduction; for in fact these costs of production include *capital* and interest, whereas our analysis of the laws of the cost of production has hitherto proceeded on the assumption that production is non-capitalistic. We should therefore be arguing in a circle [87 p. 149].

Wicksell thus finds that the use of prices to calculate values is not logically sound, and falls back on the one common element in all capital-goods, 'the importance of the time element in production . . . which distinguishes capital from land and labour and which difference is sufficient to justify the establishment of a special category of means of production, side by side with labour and land, under the name of capital' [87 p. 150] (in [86] Wicksell had still used the concept of a period of production to represent the capitalistic nature of production). Thus, 'Capital is saved-up labour and saved-up land. Interest is the difference between the marginal productivity of saved-up labour and land and of current labour and land' [87 p. 154]. This echoes Ricardo in taking labour in combination with another factor (for Ricardo it was labour and capital) and stays to a certain extent within the Austrian tradition of looking at labour and land as the 'original factors', but approximates Clark and Walras in looking at the productivity of a specific thing, capital. The determination of 'saved-up labour and land' does not seem, however, to escape from the difficulties that

Wicksell found in the average period of production (when he does work with this concept Wicksell assumes that there is 'constant taking up', i.e. that input requirements are uniform and constant over time, thus a simple average is sufficient and indeed (cf. p. 26 above) there is no substantial difference between absolute and average periods).

Concerning this difficulty Wicksell says that prices can, for analytical purposes, be taken as given when production and distribution are being considered, just as quantities of produced goods are considered as given when exchange and prices are being considered [87 pp. 102–3]. 'This procedure is equivalent to treating the problem of production (and distribution) on the assumption that only one commodity is produced – and yet even this case is complicated enough' [87 p. 243, 86 p. 153].

In general, Wicksell accepted the proposition that an increase in capital would be accompanied by an increase in product and a lower return to capital, but he seems not to exclude other possibilities: 'We have already remarked that an increase in capital need not in this case necessarily lead to an increase in *both* wages and rent. . . . On the other hand, it appears inconceivable *a priori* that an increase of capital could, *ceteris paribus*, coincide with a decrease of both wages and rent – though the question should perhaps be further investigated' [87 p. 183]. Thus Wicksell alone of all writers who found the return to capital justified by its ability to increase output, but at a diminishing rate which would cause the return to capital to fall with its continued increase, admits the possibility that the return to capital may rise and wages and consumption fall with an increase in capital and output. Thus Wicksell provides a blending of Clark, Walras and the Austrian theories, maintaining on the one hand that only man and nature are the original productive factors, 'But the productivity of both becomes, or at any rate may become, greater if they are employed for more distant ends than if they are employed for the immediate production of commodities' [87 p. 150] (with diminishing returns taken for granted), and that this difference in productivity could be attributed to a third factor of production, called capital. Recognising that this factor cannot be treated meaningfully as an aggregate Wicksell retreats into a combination of the static theory of Walras [85], Wicksteed [88] and Clark (which he calls cross-sectional) and the Austrian theory (longitudinal) [87 p. 236], to try to present an analysis of capital that is free from the flaws of both approaches.

FISHER

Irving Fisher's approach to the inclusion of time is simpler because it is not involved with the idea of time in production. Fisher distinguishes between a point in time and a period of time and thereby cuts through many definitional perplexities surrounding what should and should not be considered as capital. Thus, 'A *stock of wealth* existing at an instant of time is called *capital*. A *flow of* [abstract] *services* through a *period* of time is called *income*' [20 p. 52]. Thus, capital is anything and everything that produces income.

Although Fisher accepts the Classical conception of labour being at the root of capital and its accumulation ('we find the only ultimate item of cost to be labor cost, or, if the term "labor" be not itself sufficiently broad, labor, anxiety, trouble, annoyance, and all the other subjective experiences of an undesirable nature which are necessary in order that experiences of an agreeable nature may be secured' [20 p. 175]). He rejects the causation of the Classics, basing his system on utility. Time thus enters the system in a different way.

In order to clarify the position concerning the physical nature of capital and the value of capital-goods, Fisher identifies four basic income–capital ratios [20 p. 186].

(1) Physical productivity: quantity of services per unit of time/quantity of capital.

(2) Value productivity: value of services per unit of time/quantity of capital.

(3) Physical return: quantity of services per unit of time/value of capital.

(4) Value return: value of services per unit of time/value of capital.

As far as Fisher is concerned only the fourth ratio is of interest as having a specific meaning in the study of capital (also implying that controversy could be avoided if one identified ratios properly),

The fundamental principle which applies here is that the value of capital at any instant is derived from the value of the future income which that capital is expected to yield. The expected services may, of course, not be the actual services. In our ignorance of the future we fix our present valuations on the basis of what we expect the future to be'. 'The principle of present worth is of fundamental importance in the theory of value and prices. It means that the value of any article of wealth or property is dependent alone on the future, not the past' [20 p. 188].

Fisher looks on the definition of capital as a trivial matter once the distinction between stocks and flows is made. Since present values turn future flows into present stocks, the determination of present values gives not only a theory of price, but an indisputable method of determining capital value. Thus, for example, 'by trial and error the labor and other costs will, under normal conditions, gradually be fitted to the prices' [20 p. 189] which are determined by discounting uncertain values from an unknown future (it may be useful to point out that Fisher was as vehement as Keynes about the inherent difficulties involved with uncertainty, cf. [20 pp. 266–9]). But to avoid the problems associated with uncertainty 'we assume that expected income is foreknown with certainty and the rate of interest is foreknown' [20 p. 202].

But since the overall rate of interest requires that the prices calculated stand in a certain relation one to the others, this means that ratios 2 3 and 4 above must be distinguished on an individual and aggregate basis.

We thus need to distinguish between interest expressed in terms of money and interest expressed in terms of other goods. But no two forms of goods can be expected to maintain an absolutely constant price ratio towards each other. *There are, therefore, theoretically just as many rates of interest expressed in terms of goods as there are kinds of goods diverging from one another in value* [21 p. 42].

(It would appear obvious that Fisher was interested in determining both micro and aggregate rates of interest.) But, it is the value return that is important in defining the value of capital through the discounting procedure, and which must be determined before the distinction between capital and income can be complete.

Here Fisher follows Böhm-Bawerk (cf. p. 32 above) and looks at the rate of interest as a link between the present and future utility of a good, assuming that present goods will have a higher utility than future goods:

> This premium, that is, the terms of exchange of this year's income and next year's, may be said to depend, in brief, on the relative supply and demand of those two portions of the income stream; and this statement may be interpreted as including almost the entire impatience and investment opportunity theory of this book. But, like many brief statements, this supply and demand statement is crude and inadequate [21 p. 46].

We note, however, that the scene has shifted from the supply of future goods (labour) meeting the demand for them (capital) to a position where all individuals have both present goods (current income) and future goods (next year's income).

Just as the demand for goods at a point in time is determined by the ratios of marginal utilities to prices, Fisher extends this concept to goods at different points in time. The marginal rate of substitution read off the indifference curves becomes the 'terms of time exchanges' [21 p. 199] or the rate at which the consumer is willing to substitute present for future income (cf. Fig. 1 where *II* shows the consumer's indifference curve for present and future income). The budget line thus represents the income that could be made available, in the present or the future, if one borrowed or lent at the ruling interest rate (and not today's income as in the traditional approach). The budget line then implies a given rate of interest for it shows the rate at which today's income can be translated into future income and the rate at which future income can be translated into present consumption (represented by the line *AA'*).

But this is not the only way that income can be transferred through time. One could also invest it in a physical investment project. Thus, an individual has two possibilities; he may invest

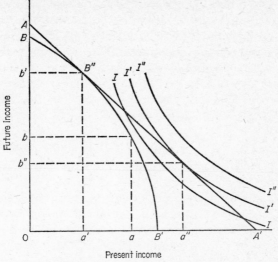

Fɪɢ. 1   Fisher's interest theory

or lend (or borrow) or both. The future return that can be
gained from a present investment opportunity is shown by the
BB' curve in the figure, and its shape suggests that there are
diminishing returns to investment opportunities. Taking all these
possibilities into account Fisher says that impatience for income
(or time preference) depends on the size of income, its time
distribution, and the probability of its occurring at the expected
times and places. All these things are reflected in the *II* curve
for the individual. Impatience can be changed, or approximated, by borrowing or lending at interest (what Fisher calls
the first approximation) as well as by investing in a physical
process of production with a positive return (the second
approximation). (Note that Fisher need no longer worry about
why capital earns a return for he has defined it as the abstract
utility services of all goods.) The final set of decisions that are
taken by individuals will determine the supply and demand
position in the money market and in the investment market
which will determine both the rate of interest and the rate of
return to investment. Since both will represent the relative
price of present to future goods this must be, in equilibrium,
equal to the rate of time preference. Thus, an individual with

45

$0a$ of present income and $0b$ of future income can increase his total income by giving up $a'a$ of his present income and investing it for a return of bb' in future income, moving himself to point B'' on the opportunity curve. Thus, he gives up $0a - 0a'$ of present income to get $0b' - 0b$ extra future income which gives him a net gain of $bb' - a'a$. This net gain in relation to forgone present income $(a'a)$ Fisher calls the rate of return (or $(bb' - a'a)\big/\overline{(a'a)}$) over cost and represents the rate of return to capital at point B''. The individual will not go beyond point B'' because his return from additional investment will be less than he could get if he now turned to the loan market where the interest rate is given by $0A/0A' - 1$ which is equal to the rate of return over cost at B''. The problem now is to find the highest indifference curve that can be attained along AA' or the point at which the rate of time preference is equal to the rate at which income can be transferred. Thus, the individual in the diagram borrows present income of $a'a''$, giving up $b'b''$, leaving him with a final allocation of $0a''$ present income and $0b''$ future income; and the highest attainable indifference curve. Thus the determination of the position for an individual with the interest rate given. His actions produce a demand for aa'' of borrowing in the loan market. Other individuals who are wanting to lend present income will make the supply side of the market and eventually the sum of demands and supplies will fix the rate of interest; and with the rate of interest given, the rate of return over cost on investment opportunity. Thus Fisher's theory that time preference, through supply and demand in the loan market, sets the rate of interest and the rate of return to capital.

The determination is thus said to be simultaneous (in the sense, for example, of the determination of prices in competitive conditions where all producers are price takers at the market price and make decisions given that price, but their aggregate decisions form together to 'determine' what the given market price is). We must make careful note, however, that while the range of rates of return that are given in the opportunity curve are assumed to be positive, the absolute values are not explained (they exist, just as the assumption that there are diminishing returns to additional investment). It is for this reason that, as Pasinetti [57] has pointed out, Fisher cannot be said to offer a theory that explains why profit on capital exists nor one that determines what its rate will be.

But Fisher himself treated his results with great caution: 'We must, therefore, give up as a bad job any attempt to formulate completely the influences which really determine the rate of interest' [21 p. 321] because things like risk and uncertainty make the curves discontinuous. Fisher thought his theory gave a general idea of the determinants of the rate of interest as well as a general theory of value and price; interest was just the price of future goods, but this result comes from the same sort of arbitrary arrangement of time as that posited by Clark. Fisher was, however, much less sure of his relations in the face of actual events than Clark. It is a theory in which production, the major concern of most of the previous writers discussed, has disappeared almost completely from the analysis (cf. [42, 73] for a modern extension).

KEYNES

As already noted above, Keynes did not much concern himself with the problems of defining capital or explaining the existence of profit. He was, however, concerned with capital to the extent that it influenced the maintenance or attainment of full employment and to this end introduced a period of production concept far removed from the Austrian. Although he saw some similarities between Fisher's rate of return over cost and his own marginal efficiency of capital, Keynes rejected Fisher's approach because a decision to increase future income at the expense of present income (a decision to save) 'is not a substitution of future consumption-demand for present consumption-demand' [48 p. 210] but 'the potentiality of consuming an unspecified article at an unspecified time' [48 p. 211]. Fisher's theory, of course, supposes that these future decisions are made in the present such that their provision can be planned for through the proper investment, leaving employment unaffected.

In terms of capital as a factor of production Keynes says,

I sympathise with the pre-classical doctrine that everything is *produced* by *labour*, aided by what used to be called art and

47

is now called technique, by natural resources which are free or cost a rent according to their scarcity or abundance, and by the results of past labour, embodied in assets, which also command a price according to their scarcity or abundance. It is preferable to regard labour, including, of course, the personal services of the entrepreneur and his assistants, as the sole factor of production, operating in a given environment of technique, natural resources, capital equipment and effective demand . . . it is much preferable to speak of capital as having a yield over the course of its life in excess of its original cost, than as being *productive*. For the only reason why an asset offers a prospect of yielding during its life services having an aggregate value greater than its initial supply price is because it is *scarce*; and it is kept scarce because of the competition of the rate of interest on money. If capital becomes less scarce, the excess yield will diminish, without it having become less productive – at least in the physical sense [48 pp. 213–14].

This view led Keynes to reject the productivity approach to capital for, 'smelly processes command a higher reward, because people will not undertake them otherwise. So do risky processes. But we do not devise a productivity theory of smelly or risky processes as such' [48 p. 215].

Thus, Keynes rejected the efficiency of lengthy processes, maintaining that short processes could be just as efficient, in terms of minimum labour inputs, as longer processes. But he did find a sense in which the concept of a period of production could have meaning. For Keynes, the optimum period of production would be that which commences at the moment in time when people decide to save, and which would produce output at just the future date and of just the type that people desire when they decide to convert their saving into consumption. Any other period, says Keynes – no matter how much more productive it may be – will not be used, because the additional output cannot be sold for lack of demand. Thus, 'In optimum conditions, that is to say, production should be so organised as to produce in the most efficient manner compatible with delivery at dates at which consumers' demand is expected to become effective' [48 p. 215]. (This optimum, as

48

Keynes points out, might require the use of absolutely inefficient processes if the propensity to consume has fallen so low that the amount of investment required to keep full employment pushes the marginal efficiency of capital below zero, cf. [13 p. 102].) Keynes's entire book is, of course, an explanation of why a *laissez-faire* system cannot be expected to produce such an optimal period of production.

Keynes also expected the rate of return on capital to fall with the accumulation of capital, but subject to the effects of the rate of interest falling at the same rate as the decline in the marginal efficiency of capital produced by the rate of accumulation necessary to keep full employment over time. Thus, since capital is kept scarce because of the alternative of getting a return on lending money due to liquidity preference, the fall in capital's return is rather different from that predicted, for example, by Smith. For Smith, the abundance of capital caused capital to compete away its return to the benefit of higher wages. For Keynes, it is not the absolute abundance or scarcity of capital, but its relative scarcity as determined by the alternative return offered by the rate of interest, or more generally by liquidity preference, for in conditions where money had no liquidity premium and the interest rate was zero, with the given quantity of capital sufficient to 'satiate to the full the aggregate desire on the part of the public to make provision for the future' [48 p. 218] the return on capital would be zero. But in such conditions either a shift in liquidity preference or the propensity to consume would make capital scarce and its return positive without any other change in the physical goods in existence.

Thus, Keynes rejects not only the concept of capital as a factor of production, but also the notion that it is productive in any sense that is meaningful in determining its return. Capital and the period of production or degree of roundaboutness are important to Keynes to the extent that the period impinges on the level of employment (cf. [48 p. 287]). The continued accumulation of capital might or might not cause the rate of return on capital to fall, indeed it might conceivably rise under certain assumptions about the rate of interest and the propensity to consume.

AN ORTHODOX (NEOCLASSICAL) THEORY OF CAPITAL?

Above (p. 9 and p. 14) we have reproduced two statements on what the orthodox theory of capital represented in 1937 and later in the 1950s and 1960s. To what extent do they correspond to the views that have been surveyed in this chapter? In reference to the 1937 statement there is no writer that would have been willing fully to subscribe to it, yet it is fully consistent with the four points that have come to characterise the orthodox neoclassical (or neo-neoclassical) theory.

We have seen that the concept of capital as an independent factor of production comes rather late, and only in a well-articulated form in the writings of Clark and Wicksell, the latter unconvinced that it was a definable concept on an aggregate basis. Almost all writers, however, concede that an aggregate capital measure has to be made in money terms, i.e. in terms of the prices of the goods that comprise the capital stock (this is true even of the Austrians who preferred to substitute the production period of capitalistic processes for capital, and attempted to use this measure to formulate a ratio of profits to aggregate capital representative of capital's return).

The first three propositions listed above (p. 14) are in a sense common to all writers surveyed if one disregards the particular definitions of capital that each proposed. All believed that the accumulation of capital would bring increased output. All believed that the increase in capital would increase output, but at a decreasing rate, thus the rationale for profit (the extra output) would be diminishing so that the profit rate would be falling. An increase in capital was thus seen as relative to both labour and output. Wicksell and Keynes were the only writers to suggest the possibility that capital accumulation might lead to a rise in profit rates. However, as the formal analysis of most of the writers was in terms of a stationary state it was not hard to show the third proposition, for if either wages or profits were higher, then consumption would be higher. Normally it was assumed that a lower profit rate meant a higher wage rate so that wage consumption would rise on an increase in capital.

This latter concept is also supported by Fisher who looks at the amount of consumption that must be given up in the present to gain a higher future income. Here the rate of return is just the extra future consumption divided by the extra investment (present consumption forgone) which can then be shown to be equal to the final productivity of capital. The rate of interest or profit is then the price of this extra consumption and Fisher's theory joins up with the productivity theory of distribution, the fourth proposition.

The productivity (or rent) theory is also recent, being found in Clark, Walras, Wicksteed and Knight. It was also held by Wicksell, but again, subject to the problems concerning the value definition of aggregate capital (Wicksteed avoided this problem by keeping to a micro theory in physical units for capital). Clark looked at it only as a broad approximation to a theory of economic dynamics.

It would not be true to say that any one writer held strictly to all of the four propositions listed. The first three are, however, to be found as general propositions subject to qualification. Almost all would have accepted (and indeed appear to pose as an unchallengeable assumption) that capital would increase output but with eventual diminishing returns, and that these diminishing returns would eventually lead to a fall in the return to capital as accumulated capital became a larger and larger proportion of both labour and output. This increasing output must then imply increased consumption (but for whom is not always specified, cf. [77]) as none countenanced increasing investment and growth, all either looking to (or arbitrarily creating) a stationary (static) equilibrium. The fourth point is less easy to generalise and only held sway in relatively recent discussion and was by no means fully accepted in the 1930s by a majority of economists (Hicks [37] is probably the *summum* of this proposition).

Two additional points of importance should also be noted before moving on to the current debates. First, the shift in the type of analysis that occurs when a concept such as Clark's imaginary static state is introduced. The system is looked at in an imposed state of rest to determine a static equilibrium. Wicksteed and Walras refined this method to the extreme and as a result, changed the essential questions posed in economics from those of the Classics to the determination of the optimal allocation of given resources. Thus, this shift in method of

51

analysis introduces another quite separate reason to have a defined measure of the capital stock, for if it is to be taken as a given quantity one must have a measure for it. The Classics, of course, were free from this particular requirement.

The second point is that in these static-type equilibriums there is no possibility for unemployment. Keynes's implied criticism of Fisher is ignored in such systems, for we always imagine, as with Clark, that the capital stock can be transmuted into the form that is appropriate to full employment.

3 Prices and Values in Systems of Production

The current revival of interest in and controversy about capital theory has been primarily concerned with the measurement of capital in value terms as implied by the four propositions concerning the return to capital and capital intensity given above (p. 14). In investigating these relations most writers use simplified examples of systems of production (stemming either from [78] or [38] – difference between the two approaches are highlighted in [1]). In this chapter we shall use a simplified system of production (taken from [78]) where commodity outputs are produced by commodity inputs (non-labour means of production) and labour. In addition, we shall use numerical examples to try to highlight the basic propositions that have been derived from the study of such systems. We must keep in mind, however, that these simple examples are not meant to be realistic representations of real economies, but only representative of the relations observed in real systems.

SIMPLE REPRODUCTION

The production of output requires the use of inputs, in specified quantities, to produce certain quantities of a specific output. The specification of the kinds and amounts of inputs required to produce any given output can be called a *process* of production. The process representing the production of, say, wheat might be written as

$$280 \text{ tons wheat} + 12 \text{ tons iron} \rightarrow 400 \text{ tons wheat},$$

i.e. it takes 280 tons of wheat and 12 tons of iron over a given period of time (say a year) to produce 400 tons of wheat.

Unless the required input of iron appears costlessly, the analysis of the production of wheat would also require a relation indicating the process used in the production of the iron that was required by the producers of wheat. Thus, the two processes for the production of wheat and iron form a *production system* which could be written as

280 tons wheat + 12 tons iron → 400 tons wheat,
120 tons wheat + 8 tons iron → 20 tons iron.

We then have a *system* of production, composed of two *processes*, that describes the amount of non-labour means of production required for a specified quantity of each output produced. The two processes of production that we have written down, when taken together with the quantities of labour required for each production cycle, we shall call a *technique of production*, or production at a given state of technical knowledge:

280 tons wheat + 12 tons iron + 2 man years → 400 tons wheat,
120 tons wheat + 8 tons iron + 1 man year → 20 tons iron.

The system presented is interdependent (or indecomposable [52]) in that the output of each process is an input in the production of the other output (as well as in its own production). The system as presented also satisfies what we shall call the condition of *self-replacement* or simple reproduction. We have assumed that the time required to produce both outputs is the same (a year) so that at the end of a production cycle each process will have produced enough product to replace the amount of that product that has been used as an input in the system taken as a whole (all non-labour inputs are assumed to be used up during the production process and thus have to be entirely replaced each year – thus this type of model is called a *circulating* capital model, for no non-labour inputs last for more than one period as would be the case in a *fixed* capital model). The outputs of the present cycle of production would then be just sufficient to satisfy the physical input needs of the next cycle. The same processes, at the same levels of activity, could then be repeated indefinitely without change in the quantities produced and without reliance on inputs from outside the system. (To simplify the development of the argument we shall omit the labour inputs in the next two sections, concentrating on the non-labour inputs.)

To aid the further analysis of such systems it will be useful to have a method of standardisation, a common denominator that will allow us to talk about the composite of inputs and outputs, and to add and subtract them. In any actual economy this function is performed by money prices which are used to convert diverse quantities to common values. We thus add the price of wheat p_w and the price of iron p_i to our system which then becomes (we also drop the units for simplification)

$$280p_w + 12p_i = 400p_w,$$
$$120p_w + 8p_i = 20p_i.$$

In the following discussion we shall be especially interested in the price of wheat in relation to the price of iron, or in the relative prices of the system. To derive relative prices without the necessity of introducing monetary relations we can use the price of wheat as a *numeraire* so that the price of iron is then denominated in terms of units of wheat instead of in units of money (or we could add a process for the production of, say, gold, with the price of both wheat and iron measured in terms of gold units). Thus, the price of wheat in terms of itself is $p_w/p_w = 1$ and the price of iron in terms of wheat is $p_{iw} = p_i/p_w$ (or, with iron as the *numeraire*, $p_i/p_i = 1$ and $p_{wi} = p_w/p_i$ with wheat measured in terms of units of iron).

We thus have a measure, wheat, which can be used to standardise the non-labour means of production in the system. Given the relative price or conversion ratio of iron into wheat we could convert all the iron quantities into their equivalent values in terms of wheat. But what will this conversion ratio, or relative price of iron in terms of wheat, be? We have already noted that a self-replacing system in a state of simple reproduction has no net output, but that it produces as outputs just what it requires as inputs for an additional cycle. Once we have introduced exchange ratios in terms of relative prices this very general condition must be made more specific. The wheat process requires 12 tons of iron as inputs. That they will be available is obvious, the real question is, will the wheat producer be able to buy them at the relative price between wheat and iron? In our example the wheat process produces 400 tons of wheat, of which 280 tons are needed as own inputs for the next production cycle. There remain 120 tons as excess to own needs which will be available to procure the required 12 tons of iron used up in the production of wheat. Up to 120 tons of wheat are then available to pay for 12 tons of iron, or 10 tons of wheat for each ton of iron. If the cost of iron is more than this the wheat producers could not purchase the iron required to start the next production cycle on the same level.

For the iron process there are 12 tons of iron surplus to own needs and the wheat input requirement is 120 tons so that iron producers will be just willing to pay 1 ton of iron for 10 tons of wheat. Thus, the first (input-replacement) condition, considered in terms of prices, is that the exchange ratio must allow each producer to procure, at that price ratio, his physical input requirements (to replace his used-up inputs).

Once the exchange ratio that meets this condition is established it can then be used as the *numeraire* to convert the system into uniform units. If we take all the iron quantities and multiply them by p_{iw} (wheat quantities, multiplied by p_w/p_w will remain unchanged) we can write them in terms of their wheat value-equivalents. When $p_{iw} = 10$ the system can be expressed wholly in terms of wheat values, W:

$$280W + 120W = 400W \quad \text{(12 iron multiplied by } p_{iw} = 120W)$$
$$120W + 80W = 200W \quad (8p_{iw} = 80W, 20p_{iw} = 200W)$$
$$\overline{400W + 200W = 600W.}$$

The total physical product of the system (400 tons wheat and 20 tons iron) can now be represented by a single sum of value measured in wheat value-equivalents, $600W$. We can check that the conversion ratio satisfies the input replacement condition by noting that the value of total inputs equals the value of total output, and that the value of inputs for each process equals the value of output. Thus, the value of the excess iron units to the value of own-requirements in iron production $(200W - 80W = 120W)$ is just equal to the cost of the wheat that is required for the replacement of wheat used up in iron production. The iron producers can thus exchange 12 tons of iron, each ton worth 10 tons of wheat, for 120 tons of wheat which is the required input. (It is easy to see that the same procedure could have been carried out in terms of iron value-equivalents by dividing the wheat value-equivalents by 10.)

EXPANDED REPRODUCTION

If the wheat process had produced, say, 575 tons of wheat instead of 400, there would be a surplus or excess on the overall input requirements for the system's next cycle of production. When the system is capable of producing a surplus in excess of its total input needs a second condition must be imposed on relative prices. We now assume that the economy is represented by a system of production such as

280 tons wheat + 12 tons iron → 575 tons wheat,
120 tons wheat + 8 tons iron → 20 tons iron.

Here the output of iron is sufficient to replace the required inputs of iron in the two processes but the total output of wheat (575 tons) exceeds the input requirements of the system (400 tons) by 175 tons of wheat which represents the net surplus or net product of the system taken as a whole. The price ratio that satisfied the first condition for the example of the self-replacing system is now no longer unique, but will lie between the limits 120 wheat/12 iron and 295 wheat/12 iron.

With the first ratio the iron producers get the required 120 tons of wheat at a cost of 12 tons of iron, the iron required as input for the production of wheat. This would leave the entire surplus of 175 tons of wheat to the wheat producers. At the other limiting ratio the input replacement condition is still satisfied, but the iron producers possess the entire surplus of wheat. Thus we need a second condition on prices to effectuate the division of the surplus among the producers. We need a rule by which the surplus is to be distributed. In a capitalist system that rule is taken to be that competitive conditions establish prices such that the rates of profits for producing each output are driven to equality, i.e. the surplus received should be the same proportion of the value of non-labour inputs in all processes. Since it is the value of the price ratio that determines who gets what proportion of the surplus we must find a price between the two limits that leaves each producer with a quantity of wheat which, as a proportion of the value of its non-labour inputs *valued at this price*, gives a uniform ratio of surplus to non-labour inputs, or uniform rate of profits. Thus, the second condition (uniform profit rates) will be satisfied by an exchange ratio that transforms the system into a common *numeraire* and distributes the surplus amongst the producers such that the ratio of the surplus of each to the value of the non-labour inputs of each calculated at this price is the same for each producer. The system must thus be written

$$(280p_w + 12p_i)\ (1 + r_w) = 575p_w,$$
$$(120p_w + 8p_i)\ (1 + r_i)\ = 20p_i,$$

and p_{iw} must be consistent with $r_w = r_i$, uniform profit rates. Solving this system for p_{iw} yields a price ratio of 15/1, which converts the entire system into wheat value-equivalents of

$$\begin{array}{l} 280W + 180W = 575W \\ 120W + 120W = 300W \\ \hline 400W + 300W = 700W + 175W \text{ (surplus).} \end{array}$$

In the production of wheat the value of the inputs of wheat and iron has a wheat value-equivalent of $(280W + 180W =)$ $460W$ which is less than the value of total wheat output $(575W)$ by $115W$ which represents the surplus or profit accruing to wheat production. In the iron process the wheat value-equivalents of the inputs of wheat and iron is $(120W + 120W =)$ $240W$ which is less than the wheat value-equivalents of the 20 tons of iron by $(300W - 240W =)$ $60W$ which is the surplus or profit on iron production. The ratio of surplus output to the value of inputs in the production of wheat is then $115W/460W$, and in the iron process, $60W/240W$. Both these ratios reduce to 1/4. In each process the surplus in wheat value-equivalents represents 25 per cent of the value of inputs all calculated at a price ratio of 15 tons of wheat equals 1 ton of iron (this ratio of surplus to inputs we might call the maximum profit or reproduction ratio, R, cf. [78], for it represents the greatest surplus available for profit after the replacement of inputs).

Since 15/1 lies between 10/1 and 295/12 we know this value of p_{iw} will satisfy the first condition on prices. The two conditions on prices in a system that produces a surplus are then (1) that they must allow replacements of inputs at the ruling price ratio; and (2) that they must distribute the surplus to all processes in uniform proportion to the value of inputs calculated at the ruling price ratio, i.e. $r_i = r_w$. These two conditions would lead us to expect that relative prices would be influenced by differences in the processes of production used in any system of production. The system satisfying our two conditions is then

$$(280W + 180W)\ (1 + 0.25) = 575W$$
$$(120W + 120W)\ (1 + 0.25) = 300W$$
$$\overline{(400W + 300W)\ (1 + 0.25) = 875W} \quad \text{for } p_{iw} = 15W.$$

LABOUR AND PRODUCTION

We are now ready to re-introduce labour as an input in production to see how this affects the values and prices in our simple system. We thus introduce for each process the quantity of labour, l, required during the production period, paid in terms of wheat units, w, per production period. Thus the wage is viewed as a deduction from the total net surplus that was, in the previous section, distributed wholly as profits at a uniform rate. The introduction of the wage in this manner will then directly affect profits, for it affects the amount of the total surplus that is available to be distributed as profits.[1] Note that we have said that the payment of positive wages will be expected to affect profits rather than the profit rate, for the profit rate is a ratio of profits to the value of inputs and the value of inputs depends on the price ratio used to calculate the inputs in equivalent values. This accounts for our interest in the value of the price ratio.

[1] The physical requirements of production are independent of the assumptions that are made about the determination of wages and the institutional arrangements for payment, but the financing of production and the determination of prices will not be. It is sufficient for our purposes to assume that wages are given (cf. [64] on the relation between the several possible assumptions ranging from strict subsistence to 'power'). If wages are paid before the production cycle they must enter as capital advanced just as expenditure on any other inputs, thereby affecting the calculation of the ratio of profit to capital advanced. Our assumption of payment after the cycle simplifies the analysis without altering the general results; both assumptions appear in the literature, the second being the more common (cf. [78, 65]).

Would it be possible for wages to take part of the surplus (thus leaving less to be paid as profit) without changing the value of p_{iw}? The answer is yes, but only under some very special conditions, so we shall deal with that case first to find out what the special restrictions are. We start by assuming that the production of wheat requires 46 man years of labour and the iron process 24 man years.

On the assumption that wages, w, are paid in wheat after the completion of the production cycle, the return or profit on the value of non-labour inputs invested over the cycle can then be calculated on the value of wheat and iron advanced during the cycle. As before, writing r for this percentage return the entire output of the system should be exhausted by (1) the replacement of inputs; (2) the payment of part of the surplus as wages $(46w + 24w = 70w)$; and (3) the remaining surplus paid as profit at some rate r on the value of the non-labour means of production $(r(400p_w + 20p_{iw})$, which, if our proposed unchanged value of $p_{iw} = 15W$ is met, becomes $r(700W))$. Thus, on the presumption of $p_{iw} = 15W$ we could write the system with the inclusion of labour as System I:

Inputs	Wages	Profits	Value of output
$(280 + 180) +$	$46lw$	$+ r(280 + 180)$	$= 575W$
$(120 + 120) +$	$24lw$	$+ r(120 + 120)$	$= 300W$
$(400 + 300) +$	$70lw$	$+ r(400 + 300)$	$= 875W$

where the values of w and r will depend on the proportion of the surplus that is claimed as payments for wages and as payments for profits, subject to the condition that $70w + r(700W) = 175W$ (and that r and w are the same in both processes at $p_{iw} = 15W$), i.e. that wages and profits cannot exceed the value of the net product available to be distributed.

We have already seen that if the whole surplus $(175W)$ is paid as profits the value of r, required to be uniform in both processes, is equal to the rate of surplus, R, for the system taken as a whole or 25 per cent $(175W/700W)$. The determination of R, carried out before the direct introduction of wages, is then similar to looking at the system with wages, but on the assumption that wages are hypothetically zero, $w = 0$, which then gives us the maximum limit to the profit rate.

WAGES AND PROFITS

If we now assume that wages are paid in positive amounts from the available surplus it then follows that the sum available to be paid as profits will be diminished from that amount which produced $r = 0.25$. With w positive we will have a system of two processes to solve for the values of w, r, p_w and p_i. Since we have made $p_w/p_w = 1$, that leaves w, r and p_{iw} ($= p_i/p_w$). In other words, since r is no longer automatically equal to R when w is positive, we need an additional equation to determine either r or w; or we can choose one of them to be given exogenously (the additional relation used to determine r is where the controversies over capital theory join those over the theory of growth [50]).

If we decide to take either r or w as exogenous, what values could they conceivably take? First, we know they will be related for we have $r(700) + (70l)w = 175W$ as a condition of the system. Further, we know that when $w = 0$ the value of $r = R = 25$ per cent. This gives a maximum value for r that the system can obtain without 'consuming its capital', i.e. assuring the input replacement condition is met. We thus have a limit that says, when $w = 0$, $r = 25$ per cent.

This suggests the other natural limit, i.e. when the whole surplus goes to wages so that profits are zero. Thus, $r = 0$ when the 70 units of labour divide the $175W$ of surplus equally, or $w = 175W/70l = 2.5W$. We then have values for the maximum and minimum values of w and r, given the physical production processes of System I which produces $R = 25$ per cent. It would then be possible to trace out all the possible intermediate combinations of w and r, taking one as exogenous, which thus determines the division of the surplus between wages and profits. A sample of these values are given in Table 2, along with values of the non-labour means of production (which, following convention, we symbolise by K), and the ratio of non-labour means of production to labour ($K/L = k$), and p_{iw}.

From the entries in Table 2 we could graph the relation between the various combinations of r and w. On the y axis we measure the wage rate w, and on the x axis the rate of profit r. The intercept on the wage axis will be, for System I, $2.5W$, and the maximum value of $r = 0.25$ will be the intercept on the r

Table 2
(in wheat value-equivalents)

	r	w	wages (wL)	profits (rK)	$wL+rK$	p_{1w}	K	k (K/L)
W	0·25	0	0	115	115	1·0	460	10
I	0·25	0	0	60	60	15·0	240	10
W	0·20	0·5	23	92	115	1·0	460	10
I	0·20	0·5	12	48	60	15·0	240	10
W	0·15	1·0	46	69	115	1·0	460	10
I	0·15	1·0	24	36	60	15·0	240	10
W	0·10	1·5	69	46	115	1·0	460	10
I	0·10	1·5	36	24	60	15·0	240	10
W	0·05	2·0	92	23	115	1·0	460	10
I	0·05	2·0	48	12	60	15·0	240	10
W	0	2·5	115	0	115	1·0	460	10
I	0	2·5	60	0	60	15·0	240	10

axis. By plotting the intermediate values we see that the relation is a straight line of the form $w = 2\cdot5 - 10r$ or $r = 0\cdot25 - 0\cdot1w$, depending on whether w or r is taken as exogenous (Fig. 2).

Inspection of Table 2 indicates that we have been able to consider different divisions of the surplus between wages and profits with the same price ratio satisfying the stipulated conditions on prices. As we expected we also find that when the value of p_{1w} is unchanging the values of the non-labour means of production used in the system will be constant (refer to columns

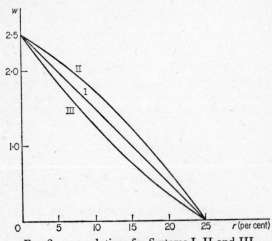

FIG. 2 *w–r* relations for Systems I, II and III

K and k). We must now enquire into the special conditions that were necessary for this result and try to understand why it came about.

PRICES AND CAPITAL VALUES

To investigate the relation between differences in r and w and constancy in p_{iw} and K let us look more closely at the price ratio. We could solve the wheat process equation for p_{iw} by taking the maximum value of w when $r=0$ as $2 \cdot 5W$ as follows:

$$(280W + 12p_{iw})\ (1+0) + 46l(2 \cdot 5W) = 575W,$$
$$(280W + 12p_{iw})\ (1+0) + 115W = 575W,$$
$$12p_{iw} = 575W - (115W + 280W) = 180W,$$
$$p_{iw} = 15W \quad (p_{ww} = 1W).$$

This price ratio then served to convert the system into common wheat value-equivalents. This conversion gave $(280W + 180W = 460W)$ and $(120W + 120W = 240W)$ as the values of the non-labour means of production in the wheat and iron process respectively. As long as p_{iw} is unchanged with differences in w and r, it follows that there will be no change in the values of the non-labour means of production. This is the case in System I as shown by Table 2, columns p_{iw} and K. If we were to plot the value of the combined non-labour means of production used in System I in relation to r, it would be the vertical line at $700W$ shown in Fig. 3 (p. 67).

A closer look at the rK and wL columns of Table 2 may help us to understand why this result occurs. Consider the effect on the wheat process of a change in w from $2 \cdot 5$ to $1 \cdot 0$. The wage bill, wL, will be reduced from $wL = 115$ to $wL = 46$. In the iron process the difference in the wage bill is from $60W$ to $24W$. We notice that in both the difference is of the same percentage amount, 60 per cent, i.e. costs of production represented by wages fall in the same proportion in both processes. If only the lower wage were taken into account the price in both processes could fall by the same proportion without impairing the ability to pay the new lower wage bill out of receipts at lower prices.

But, at the same time that w is lower, r will be higher and profit must now be calculated at a rate of 15 per cent on the non-labour means of production. The necessity of paying profits at the higher rate will work against the potential decrease in price so that prices could not fall by the full percentage of the savings on the wages bill. Table 2 tells us that $115W$ and $60W$ would be sufficient to meet profit at a rate of 15 per cent on the value of the non-labour means of production in the wheat and iron process respectively. These amounts, however, are just equal to the savings on the payment of lower wages. Prices then cannot fall, indeed, they cannot change at all for the total revenue generated at the old prices is just sufficient to pay the new lower rate of wages, with the savings on wages being just taken up by the necessity to pay the new higher rate of profits.

The reason for the unchanged price ratio may become more obvious if we look at the proportions in which labour and non-labour means of production are combined in the two processes for it is this proportion which determines the proportions by which the wages bill falls and the profits requirement rises as w and r differ. If, for example, the wheat process had required more labour, its savings from a given reduction in the wage rate would have been greater. It would then have had more than required to pay profit at the new rate. Price would then have had to fall to eliminate this extra profit and bring the rate of profit back into uniformity. In such a case the old price ratio would no longer have satisfied the condition concerning uniform profit rates. The price of wheat in terms of iron would have to fall in order to bring the profit rate to uniformity between processes. The opposite would have been the case if the iron sector had used more labour (subject to the condition that the means of production themselves were produced by the same processes, etc., cf. [78 pp. 14–15]). The special restriction that we have been seeking is then associated with uniformity in the proportions of non-labour means of production to labour in the processes.

To see the force of this restriction we now assume that the wheat process requires more of the 70 units of labour and the iron sector less, giving System II:

$$(280 \text{ wheat} + 12 \text{ iron } p_{iw}) \ (1+r) + 60lw = 575 \text{ wheat,}$$
$$(120 \text{ wheat} + 8 \text{ iron } p_{iw}) \quad (1+r) + 10lw = 20 \text{ iron } p_{iw}.$$

With $r = 0$ and $w = 2.5$ we can solve again for p_{iw}:

$$(280 + 12p_{iw}) \ (1+0) + 60l.2 \cdot 5W = 575,$$
$$(120 + 8p_{iw}) \quad (1+0) + 10l.2 \cdot 5W = 20p_{iw},$$

to find that $p_{iw} = 12 \cdot 08W$, which gives us the ratio that converts System II into wheat value-equivalents on the basis of 1 iron $= 12 \cdot 08$ wheat:

$$(280W + 144 \cdot 96W) \ (1+r) + 150W = 575W$$
$$(120W + 96 \cdot 64W) \ (1+r) + 25W \ = 241 \cdot 6W$$
$$\overline{(400W + 241 \cdot 6W) \ (1+r) + 175W = 816 \cdot 6W}$$

and we find that the value of the non-labour means of production is now only $641 \cdot 6W$ as compared with $700W$ in the case of System I.

Similarly, we can calculate the maximum value of $r = R$ by setting $w = 0$. Since we are working with the same physical processes with the same total quantities of inputs and outputs as System I it follows that the maximum reproduction rate will be unchanged and thus the maximum $r = R$ is still 25 per cent. It also follows that the relative prices that ruled when $w = 0$ will still rule, for with $w = 0$ the change in labour requirement is cancelled out (i.e. it is as if there were no labour) so $p_{iw} = 15W$. Thus, the limiting values of w and r will be undisturbed by the new labour requirements; the maximum w is still $2 \cdot 5W$ and the maximum r is 25 per cent. But, as may now be apparent, the intermediate combinations of w and r will not be the same. A hint that this will be so can be seen from the fact that the value of p_{iw} at $r = 0$ and the value of non-labour means of production are not the same as they were in the previous case. Table 3 (p. 66) gives the w–r values for System II.

The alternative possibility would be to have reversed the amounts of labour required in each process, forming System III as

$$(280 \text{ wheat} + 12 \text{ iron } p_{iw}) \ (1+r) + 10lw = 575 \text{ wheat,}$$
$$(120 \text{ wheat} + 8 \text{ iron } p_{iw}) \quad (1+r) + 60lw = 20 \text{ iron } p_{iw}.$$

Table 3
(in wheat value-equivalents)

	r	w	wages (wL)	profits (rK)	$wL+rK$	p_{iw}	K	k (K/L)
W	0·25	0	0	115·00	115·00	1·00	460·00	7·66
I	0·25	0	0	60·00	60·00	15·00	240·00	24·00
W	0·20	0·5365	32·190	90·47	122·66	1·00	452·34	7·54
I	0·20	0·5365	5·365	46·98	52·34	14·36	234·90	23·49
W	0·15	1·0535	63·210	66·76	129·97	1·00	445·04	7·42
I	0·15	1·0535	10·535	34·51	45·03	13·75	230·05	23·01
W	0·10	1·5522	93·120	43·80	136·94	1·00	438·06	7·30
I	0·10	1·5522	15·522	22·54	38·06	13·17	225·37	22·54
W	0·05	2·0300	122·046	21·60	143·31	1·00	431·38	7·19
I	0·05	2·0300	20·341	11·05	31·39	12·62	220·92	22·09
W	0·00	2·5000	150·000	00·00	150·00	1·00	424·99	7·08
I	0·00	2·5000	25·000	00·00	25·00	12·08	216·66	21·67

Table 4 shows the range of w–r and associated values for System III. The w–r relations are drawn up for all three systems in Fig. 2 where we see that the curve for System II lies

Table 4
(in wheat value-equivalents)

	r	w	wages (wL)	profits (rK)	$wL+rK$	p_{iw}	K	k (K/L)
W	0·25	0·0000	0·000	115·00	115·00	1·00	460·00	46·00
I	0·25	0·0000	0·000	60·00	60·00	15·00	240·00	4·00
W	0·20	0·4256	4·256	95·12	99·38	1·00	475·62	47·56
I	0·20	0·4256	25·536	50·08	75·62	16·30	250·41	4·17
W	0·15	0·8846	8·846	73·85	82·70	1·00	492·31	49·23
I	0·15	0·8846	53·076	39·23	92·38	17·69	261·54	4·36
W	0·10	1·3806	13·806	51·02	64·80	1·00	510·18	52·94
I	0·10	1·3806	82·836	27·35	110·20	19·18	273·45	4·55
W	0·05	1·9174	19·174	26·47	45·64	1·00	529·36	52·94
I	0·05	1·9174	115·044	14·31	129·36	20·78	286·24	4·77
W	0	2·5000	25·000	0	25·00	1·00	550·00	55·00
I	0	2·5000	150·000	0	150·00	22·50	300·00	5·00

everywhere above that for System I except for their common intercepts. Alternatively, the w–r relation for System III lies below that for I and II. We also note that the price changes and the changes in capital values are in different directions for Systems I and II. This can be seen in Fig. 3 where the relative prices and capital values of the three systems are drawn up in relation to the rate of profits. It thus becomes clear that our initial case of constant prices and capital values can only result

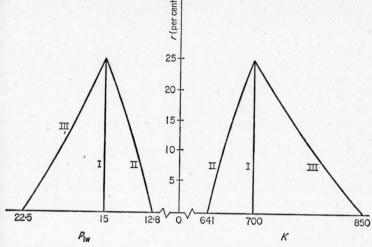

Fig. 3 K and p_{iw} values for Systems I, II and III

from the very special assumption about the proportion of non-labour means of production to labour, and will not in general occur when this restriction is not met. The straight line $w-r$ relation then becomes a special case only associated with labour requirements as given in System I. Indeed, depending on the technique of production and the number of processes involved nearly any shape of the $w-r$ relation would be possible (cf. [24 p. 264]).

In the literature these relations have a number of different names. Our System II, which has an outward bending (or bulging) shape is called a *negative price Wicksell effect* and System III, which bends (or bulges) inwards, is said to represent a *positive price Wicksell effect*, with the straight line relation of System I showing a *neutral price Wicksell effect*. This nomenclature emphasises the fact that, in general, relative prices will not be constant (nor will the value of the same physical non-labour means of production) for different combinations of w and r. This result comes as much from differences in the processes of production for outputs as from the fact that the means of production themselves are heterogeneous [75, 76]. For prices to be constant one must assume that all processes are the same or that all outputs are produced by the non-labour means of production in a given proportion with labour.

GEOMETRICAL ESTIMATION OF PRICE
WICKSELL EFFECTS

An easy method of keeping these relations in mind without having to calculate tables as we have done above is the following [2, 3, 29]. Let q be net output per unit of labour ($2 \cdot 5W$ in our examples). This output per man will be divided between w, wages per man, and the payment of profit per man for a given value of non-labour means of production per man ($r(K/L) = rk$). Thus w and r have the same meaning as in our examples and k is now the aggregate value of the k values for each process given in the tables. This relation then says that $q = w + rk$, which can be rearranged to give an expression for the value of non-labour means of production per unit of labour: $k = (q - w)/r$.

As an example, take the outward bulging curve of System II reproduced in Fig. 4. Pick two points on the curve, say $r_1 = 0 \cdot 05$

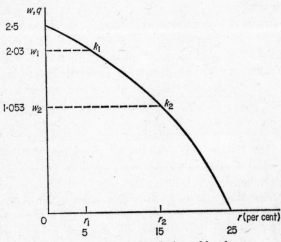

FIG. 4   Graphical calculation of k-values

and $r_2 = 0 \cdot 15$, with associated w values of $2 \cdot 03$ and $1 \cdot 053$. Now solve for k_1 at $r_1 - w_1$ and k_2 at $r_2 - w_2$. For k_1, k is equal to the distance $0q$ less the distance $0w_1$, divided by the distance $0r_1$. From Table 3 we know that the numerical values for these distances are $0q = 2 \cdot 5$, $0w_1 = 2 \cdot 03$, so that $k_1 = (2 \cdot 5 - 2 \cdot 03)/0 \cdot 05 = 9 \cdot 4$ and $k_2 = (2 \cdot 5 - 1 \cdot 053)/0 \cdot 15 = 9 \cdot 64$ (both values can be verified against the table if multiplied by 70 to give total capital value [29 p. 43]). Note that this method is strictly valid only for the case used here, i.e. one consumable net output in a stationary state. In a growing system q and w $(r=0)$ will not in general be comparable (cf. Appendix on p. 85). In this example we see that when r_1 is lower than r_2 the value of non-labour means of production per unit of labour at k_1 is less than k_2. Thus $r_1 < r_2$ implies $k_1 < k_2$ with an outward bulging curve. This is called a 'negative' price Wicksell effect because the higher rate of profit is associated with a higher value of non-labour means of production as a proportion of labour employed, which is the inverse (or negation) of the result that Wicksell expected, i.e. that 'a large amount of capital and a comparatively small number of workers will always be connected with a longer period of production, high wages and a low rate of interest – and vice versa' [86 p. 127].

CHOOSING DIFFERENT TECHNIQUES

The propositions that we have been discussing are concerned with the relations of w, r, and the value of non-labour means of production within a given technique of production. However, part of the orthodox theory concerns the combinations in which inputs are used as a function of their relative prices; the relatively more expensive input being used relatively less intensively in production and vice versa. These relative changes in inputs can be represented within the context of systems of production by drawing up a number of different production systems, each differing in its use of at least two of the required inputs, or requiring different inputs and producing different outputs (we now leave our simple numerical examples and assume that there may be any number of inputs and outputs, but remembering that there must always be at least as many processes as there are produced outputs for any given technique). This ensemble of techniques would represent what is called a book of technical engineering blueprints, where each page represents a different combination of inputs capable of producing different types of outputs.

It would then be possible, following the procedure set out

above, to calculate for each page in the book of blueprints the maximum values of w and r, and the w–r relations, as well as the relative prices for each combination of w and r. If we were to put all the w–r relations for all the techniques in the blueprint book into one diagram we would have a representation of all possible combinations of r and w, given technology.

One could then exercise a process of choice of the following nature. Given an exogenously determined value of r ruling in an economy, which of all the possible techniques would give the highest w when operated with the given r? Techniques satisfying this condition would then be superior to (or dominate) all others at that r. As an example, if we chart just three of the possible techniques (or the three standard types) in Fig. 5 we would see that at $r = 0 \rightarrow r_1$, technique a would give the highest

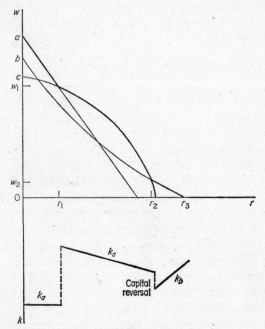

FIG. 5   Choice of alternative techniques

value of w. From $r_1 \rightarrow r_2$ technique c gives the higher w and from $r_2 \rightarrow r_3$, technique b gives the higher w. At $r = 0 \rightarrow r_1$ techniques b and c are both excluded because they have wages per man lower than a (there may also be other techniques available, but

70

because they give lower w for all values of r they are excluded). The heavy outer boundary of w–r lines thus traces the techniques that would be most profitable at values of r from 0 to r_3. As above, we can trace out the capital value of each technique below the w–r portion of the diagram. The solid line here corresponds to the values of the non-labour means of production that are chosen according to the heavy-lined w–r envelope of dominant techniques.

Now, if we enquire into the relation between differences in r and differences in k we can see that a higher r can be associated with a lower or a higher value of non-labour means of production per unit of labour. For example, at r below r_1, the value of k is k_a, while at values of r above r_1, the value of k is k_c. Here a higher r is associated with a lower k, while for r above r_2 the opposite is the case.

At $r=r_1$ we see that both techniques a and c give the same w–r value and thus, at r_1, there is nothing to recommend either technique as preferable. At values of r slightly higher or slightly lower than r_1 either a or c would be preferred. This point of equality between the two alternative techniques is called a *switch point*, or a point at which the two techniques are equi-profitable, while at any point on either side a switch from one to the other would give a higher w or r (some writers have tried to define the switch in terms of a marginal product of the switch, a concept rather different from the orthodox meaning of the term, cf. [74, 32]).

What must be determined, in relation to the orthodox theory, is whether a different value of r makes a technique that is more or less expensive in terms of the value of non-labour means of production tied up in it more or less profitable. If the switch represents a negative relation between the difference in r and the value of the non-labour means of production required for the technique then we have what is called a *forward switch* – forward because it relates a higher r to a lower k, which is again the 'expected' orthodox result. This would be the case at r_1.

Alternatively, a *backward switch* or *capital reversal* (or the Ruth Cohen 'curiosum' [61]) is the case where there is a positive relation between the difference in r and k; when r is higher k is higher, as at r_2. (Intersections below the envelope have been called *false* switches, cf. [66].) These two cases have a family

71

resemblance to the price Wicksell effects discussed above. The present relations, however, refer not to the difference in k subsequent to a different combination of r and w for a *single* technique of production, but to differences in k that are associated with *different* techniques of production. Since they relate to real differences in production techniques they are referred to as real (as opposed to price) Wicksell effects. The *positive real Wicksell effect* is thus the name given to a forward switch, and *negative real Wicksell effect* the name given to capital reversal or a backward switch.

Another phenomenon that occurs with changes in techniques of production is that techniques that may be chosen as superior at one rate of profit may be replaced by a different technique at a different rate of profit, but again become the most profitable at a third value of r. A given technique may thus come back, or give the highest w–r combination at more than one value of r, again demonstrating that there may be no general relation between r and k. This coming back or repetition is called *double switching*, as shown in Fig. 6 (cf. [4] for rules on the maximum number of switches). Here technique a is preferable at $r = 0 \rightarrow r_1$ and again at $r = r_2 \rightarrow r_3$. There are two switches in which a is involved, so we may say that there is a double switch

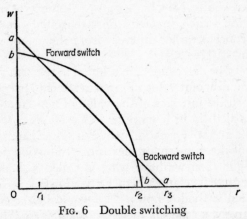

FIG. 6   Double switching

or *reswitching*, for at one switch-point a is replaced by another technique and at the second switch-point it replaces that technique which had been superior on grounds of profitability at the previous switch.

72

The terminology of these concepts is perhaps unfortunate for we continually call positive relations negative. This is because the orthodox or normal relation between r and k is thought to be negative, so this normal relation gets the approbation of expected or positive or well behaved. When this negative relation is contradicted or negated it is called a negative result or backward, perverse or badly-behaved. The results generated by the current debates suggest that there is nothing any more normal about the negative relations than the positive.

Further, the word 'switch' may suggest that there are actual changes and substitutions of techniques going on over time when indeed we are simply comparing steady or stationary states, or looking at different possible combinations at an isolated point of calendar time. One is best served to think of each point on each curve as an independent economy. Differences in w–r combinations then represent comparisons of conditions in two different economies operating under the specified difference in the internal conditions of production. One then poses a question of the form: 'What technique would rule in A if $r = r_a$ and in B if $r = r_b$, and what, if any, would be the difference in k and w between the two?' This should be clear when we remember that each relation represents a specific set of inputs specified by the blueprint of the technique. We cannot change from one set of physical production conditions to another without a process of adjustment (if at all).

We thus see that in the case of one technique and in the case of a choice between a number of techniques there may be important exceptions to the orthodox predictions about the relation between r and k. This, as we have seen, is for two basic reasons. First, because the non-labour means of production are heterogeneous they must be aggregated to derive a simple relation between capital as an aggregate factor of production and the return to this aggregate. But there is no way that an aggregate value can be created that is independent of r, except in the case of relative prices being constant. Secondly, in general goods are produced by different processes of production, and when this is the case relative prices cannot be constant. The orthodox results will only hold in the restricted case where these two conditions are not met.

THE ORTHODOX POSITION

However, suppose that we wanted to present the case where only the expected, orthodox results occurred. We know (from p. 67) that there is one condition that will rule out negative price Wicksell effects without presuming that only positive effects exist, i.e. the neutral case where the ratios of the value of non-labour means of production to labour are uniform. If we were to collect out of our book of blueprints *only* those which were neutral (let us suppose that there are a number of them) to the neglect of all others we could construct an envelope of superior neutral techniques only, as in Fig. 7. With a large number of techniques the corners would smooth out and we would have a smooth relation between r and k which was indeed negative, exactly what is required for the orthodox results. This is the result that Samuelson desired when he evoked his *Surrogate Production Function* [67] from a blueprint technology

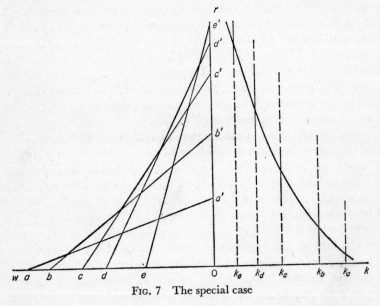

FIG. 7   The special case

(cf. [24]). We are now in a position to see what is required to achieve the orthodox result.

First, we know that the straight line w–r relation implies that relative prices are constant for all combinations of w and r. This also implies that the ratios of non-labour means of production to labour are identical (or strictly proportional, cf. [31]). This implies that the processes of production are the same for all outputs. Alternatively, one could look at this assumption as implying a system of production with only one process which produces one single output which has multiple uses (or that there is only one primeval capital good, which, like Adam, fathered all the rest).

Our case, however, differs from Samuelson's in that his derivation of the orthodox case did not use a model with circulating capital, which requires replacement each period, but fixed capital which lasts over time. Posed in this way the result requires not only that relative output prices are independent of w and r, but also that the relative prices of newly produced and partly used-up capital goods are independent of w and r. As Steedman [81] has pointed out, Samuelson's surrogate case with fixed capital will only hold when the depreciation rule that is used to calculate the value of old capital goods is independent of w and r (which, as Sraffa [78] pointed out, it will not be) or when the capital goods can be expected to last for ever.

The orthodox theory thus can be seen as a special case requiring restrictions on the structure of production that are non-existent in reality and have no obvious logical support or theoretical foundation. If these special conditions are not accepted as general then capital values and the capital intensity of any process will not be independent of the ruling rate of profits or wage rate. The determination of either the wage or the profit rate must be dealt with elsewhere than in the production technology.

THE AVERAGE PERIOD OF PRODUCTION AND CAPITAL INTENSITY

We have suggested in Chapter 2 that the approach to capital via the production function has only recent and limited relation to the historical development of orthodox doctrine. Much of this development is dominated by the view that capital can be treated as the accumulated labour time embodied in physical equipments, or the time and subsistence funds necessary for labour to convert natural resources into more productive forms. This emphasis on natural resources, labour and time is exemplified in the Austrian theory's concept of an average period of production.

This time measure of capital is derived from the average distribution of labour inputs expended over the production period. Labour inputs applied, say, 25 years ago are viewed as being embodied in production for each of the 25 years taken in production. Thus if l units of labour are used in the first year of a 25-year process the embodied cost over that year would be the wages of l labourers, wl, plus interest on that amount, $r(wl)$ or $wl + r(wl) = wl(1+r)$. After the second year of the process, the expenditure of the first year will have been embodied over two years, and its cost calculated as $\{wl + r(wl)\}(1+r)$ or $wl(1+r)^2$. At the end of the process the labour applied 25 years ago is then $wl(1+r)^{25}$. By costing up the total labour employed in each period of the process we could compare the embodied labour of two different time patterns of labour inputs.

If we take two processes, A and B, each of 25-year length and each requiring the same inputs, say one unit, in each period with the exception that A uses 20 additional units eight periods before the end of the process and B one additional unit in the first period of the process and 19 additional units in the last period of the process, their difference in cost will be caused by the difference in the twenty-fifth, eighth and last period before the end of the process or $A = 20w(1+r)^8$ and $B = 19w(1+r) + 1w(1+r)^{25}$.

The cost differences can then be seen by calculating A and B for different combinations of r and w. On the assumption that $r = 25$ per cent when $w = 0$, and $w = 1$ when $r = 0$ [cf. 78], Table 5 gives the values of A and B for several values of r.

Table 5

	00	0·05	0·10	0·15	0·20	0·25
A	20	23·6	25·7	24·5	17·19	0·00
B	20	18·7	19·0	21·9	23·6	0·00
$A - B$	00	4·9	6·7	2·6	− 6·4	0·00

76

In terms of an average period of production the two techniques would be ranked by the formula given above (p. 32) with $A_t = 19\cdot4$ and $B_t = 14\cdot76$, i.e.

$$A_t = (25 + 24 + 23 + \ldots + (21\cdot8) + 7 + 6 + \ldots + 1)/25;$$
$$B_t = (25\cdot2) + 24 + 23 + \ldots + 3 + 2 + (20\cdot1)/25.$$

A is thus more capital intensive in Böhm-Bawerk's sense for it represents a higher average investment in wages over time. At high rates of profit B should be used and at some lower r process A should be preferred. But the figures in the table show that at low rates of profit B is the cheapest and that there is no general relation between the cost of the technique and the rate of profits. The failure of the average period to vary negatively with r does not, however, mean that time is not important, but simply that the single-measure average period cannot be used as a substitute for the value of aggregate heterogeneous physical capital goods and that all technical differences in production cannot be reduced to the common denominator of time in a unique and consistent way (cf. [28]).

Although the average period has no general application and cannot avoid the problem faced by capital valuation independent of the rate of profit, the Austrian methods in themselves have become increasingly popular ([39, 40, 55], but [9, 84] offer critiques). The Austrian method, as distinct from the use of the concept of the average period (part of Nuti's [55] purpose was to demonstrate the point that the average period could not rescue orthodox theory from error – he was preceded by [23, 78]) – begins by specifying a technique in terms of its use of labour over the time period required for the construction of inputs, and then the application of labour required to operate the technique to produce output over its economic life. Thus, a technique, as the average period, is specified by the time distribution of labour inputs over the construction period and the time distribution of labour producing output over the period of actual operation.

If l represents labour input and L the time distribution of the ls over n periods $(L = \sum_n l_n)$ then the cost of construction of a technique can be expressed as $wL(1 + r)^n$, with w the wage. The net output of the technique in operation can then be expressed as q per period over m periods of operation and the time distribution of net output as Q ($= \sum_m q_m$). The present value of operating the constructed technique (as in the marginal efficiency decision) is then $Q/(1+r)^m$. Any technique put into operation must then satisfy the competitive condition that present value equals supply price or $Q/(1+r)^m = wL(1+r)^n$. Another way of putting this condition would be to look at the costs and revenues before starting the construction period and before the receipt of revenues from operating the technique over its lifetime. The present value of the construction costs is then $wL(1+r)^{-n}$ and the revenues $Q(1+r)^{-(m+n)}$. Expected revenues less expected construction costs is then $Q(1+r)^{-(m+n)} - wL(1+r)^{-n} = 0$. From this we could then derive a relation between w and r of the form $w = Q(1+r)^{-(m+n)}/L(1+r)^{-n}$ [55]. Thus, from any given pattern of q and l there will emerge a $w-r$ relation which gives the same results as our earlier examples only now production is looked at horizontally over time rather than vertically at a point in time.

The equivalent of the straight line $w-r$ relation would be a uniform flow of inputs and outputs (or Wicksell's constant taking up assumption, cf. [40, 28]). The relations can also have inward and outward bulges which will be dependent on the time pattern of the distribution of labour in construction and production. Choice between different techniques can also be handled in this formulation, just as for systems at a point in time.

SIMPLE PRODUCTION SYSTEMS AND MODELS OF PRODUCTION

The simple examples of production systems that we have used in our numerical examples stem from Sraffa, and can be symbolised more generally. If we call our input quantities (e.g. wheat and iron) by capital letters (A, B, etc.) with subscripts to indicate the process in which they are employed as inputs our simple wheat and iron system could be written:

$$(A_a p_a + B_a p_b)(1+r) + L_a w = A p_a,$$
$$(A_b p_a + B_b p_b)(1+r) + L_b w = B p_b,$$

or for as many processes as exist, provided that there is at least one process for every output and all inputs are produced in the system. In our examples we have assumed that $p_a = p_w/p_w = 1$ with $A_a + A_b < A$; $B_a + B_b = B$, i.e. that there is a surplus of outputs over inputs for the system. We have also treated L as a quantity of labour units and w as the wage rate (i.e. the share of the surplus going to labour divided by the quantity of labour). Sraffa reverses this process by assuming that $\sum L = 1$ and that w is the share of the surplus paid as wages. Thus, the two assumptions are equivalent for the numerical examples as we have set them up. The wage is viewed as being paid after the production cycle and thus does not enter as working capital for the calculation of profit rates.

A method apparently similar to Sraffa's is the use of production models as employed by Hicks [38] and Spaventa [75, 76]. In this approach output is not viewed as being produced by a number of other outputs used as inputs, but by labour and 'machines' (Hicks calls them tractors). There are two processes, one for the production of more machines and the other for consumption:

machines (m) + labour (L) → consumption goods (C),
machines (m) + labour (L) → machines (M),

which we might look at, with quantities added, as

$10M$ (machines) + $5L$ (labour) → $100C$ (consumption goods),
$40M$ (machines) + $10L$ (labour) → $50M$ (machines).

But as such models are set up under conditions of constant returns to scale in the aim of looking at changes (or traverses [38]), quantities are replaced by input coefficients per unit of output. In a system that only recognises machines and labour as inputs there will be four input coefficients, one each for labour used in the production of machines, b, and the production of consumption goods, β, and for machines used in the production of machines, a, and the production of consumption goods, α. With the quantities introduced in the example above the appropriate coefficients would be $a = 40/50 = 0\cdot8$, $b = 10/50 = 0\cdot2$, $\alpha = 10/100 = 0\cdot1$ and $\beta = 5/100 = 0\cdot05$. Thus, the model becomes:

$$aM + \beta L = C \quad \text{or} \quad 0 \cdot 1M + 0 \cdot 05L = C$$
$$aM + bL = M \qquad\qquad 0 \cdot 8M + 0 \cdot 20L = M.$$

If we let π be the price of the consumption good and p the price of the capital good we would obtain equations for the prices of consumption goods and machines as $\pi = apr + \beta w$ and $p = apr + bw$ where w and r are the wage and profit rate. (We note that r rather than $1 + r$ appears in these equations on the assumption that machines last for ever and need not be replaced – all output is thus net of replacement as there is no replacement.[1] From these equations the relative prices and the w–r relation can be derived just as we have done above by setting $\pi = 1$, giving

$$w = \frac{1 - ar}{\beta((1 + a(m-1)r)}.$$

This particular approach has unfortunately two quite separate types of substitution and composition effects. In his original presentation [38] Hicks suggests a rule for classifying the capital intensity of wage curves (w–r relations) in the following manner. From the price equations we can derive $1/w = \beta + rab/1 - ra$, which gives, with $r = 0$, the intercept of the wage curve as $w = 1/\beta$. Further manipulation of the same relation gives $(ab - a\beta)wr + \beta w + ar = 1$, which, with $w = 0$, gives the r intercept as $1/a$. Both of these limits are what could be called 'pure' coefficients for β is labour per unit of consumption (or wage) goods and a is a unit of machine per unit of machine output. Thus two intersecting w–r relations (the second denoted by a prime $'$) will always have an envelope which has a lower k associated with a higher r if $a < a'$ and $\beta > \beta'$, i.e. a lower real wage will result in a lower a and a higher β. Thus,

[1] Many fixed capital production models do assume depreciation by adding some exogenously determined proportion, d, to cover replacement. Thus, for everlasting fixed capital $d = 0$ and for circulating capital $d = 1$ $(r + d) = (1 + r)$. For intermediate values of d the relation is not so simple for the correct depreciation adjustment and the prices of partly used capital goods will be dependent on the ruling value of r (cf. [78, 44, 75, 81]) so that $(r + d)$ is not the correct expression except in the limiting cases.

for two techniques which have $m = 1$ and intersecting w–r relations it will be true that $\beta' < \beta\ (1/\beta' > 1/\beta)$ and $a' > a\ (1/a' < 1/a)$. A lower w will bring into use a technique with a higher β and a lower a. This change, with m constant, Hicks called substitution (and is associated with a negative relation between r and k).

Brown [7] expanded this suggestion by Hicks and investigated the relation between differences in a and β (substitution effects) and differences in m (which Brown calls the 'composition ratio') as representative of composition effects. The combination of the two (a, β, m) determining what Brown calls C.I.U. (capital intensity uniqueness, i.e. the orthodox result). Brown refines Hicks's approach by substituting $y = ab$ for m, thus making (a, β, y) the determinants of C.I.U., showing that if y is unchanged (a condition supposed weaker than m unchanged) then substitution effects dominate composition effects and C.I.U. holds (i.e. the relation between r and k is negative). The reader should note that these terms differ from the effects cited by Spaventa [75] and those mentioned in the Appendix, where both may exist for one given technique as well as for the case of the substitution of one technique for another. Brown's exercise is primarily concerned to demonstrate the minimum restrictions necessary for a production model to produce the orthodox results (cf. [8]) while Spaventa is concerned with rather the opposite (see also [55]).

Using production models as shown above, a technique of production can be represented by a matrix of technical coefficients of the form $\begin{bmatrix} \alpha & \beta \\ a & b \end{bmatrix}$ and a difference in any one of the coefficients would constitute a different technique (either because the composition of output would be different or the type of outputs would be different). These coefficients of production can also be used to represent the difference in capital intensity between two processes which will determine the shape of the associated w–r relation. Define m as the ratio of the machine to labour coefficients in each process: $\alpha/\beta : a/b$ or $ab/a\beta = m$. There will be a relation between m and the shape of the w–r relation for each technique. If, for example, the same process were used in both the production of machines and consumption goods, then $\alpha/\beta = a/b$ and $m = 1$, giving a straight-

81

line w–r relation. If the machine sector is relatively more machine intensive then $a/\beta < a/b$ and $m < 1$ which would give an outward bulging w–r curve (or negative price Wicksell effect). For the consumption sector more machine intensive than the machine sector $a/\beta > a/b$ and $m > 1$ with an inward bulge (positive price Wicksell effect). In our example above the value of m would be $0\cdot1/0\cdot05 : 0\cdot8/0\cdot2$ or $a/\beta < a/b$; or $ab/a\beta = 0\cdot1 \times 0\cdot2/0\cdot8 \times 0\cdot05 = 1/2$ which is less than 1 and would give an outward-bulging w–r relation.

Thus, the formal results are similar to those derived from a Sraffa-type system of production although the assumptions underlying them are rather different.

APPENDIX

In our numerical examples we have assumed that the surplus (net product) either disappeared or was fully consumed when paid as profit and wages. However, the disposition of the surplus is important as the basis of expanding the scale of production in the system. We could assume that the net product was used to increase the level of activity in each succeeding period. Looking at the system in this way would require an assumption about returns to scale, and the most common in the literature, that of constant returns, will be employed.

We have already noted that the maximum rate of surplus, R, was equal to the maximum rate of profit for the system. Since the maximum rate of expansion of the system would be where all the surplus is used for investment in increasing the scale of activity this would mean that none of the surplus could be consumed. Thus, when the rate of expansion, g, is at a maximum, consumption per head, c, will be zero, and when all the surplus is consumed, c would be at its maximum but the system would be in a stationary state with $g = 0$ (recall that the surplus is in wheat so that wheat is the wage good that is consumed). Just as we had maximum and minimum limits for w and r we will have corresponding limits for c and g.

The system set out in the examples is only compatible with $g = 0$ for it produces only enough iron for replacement of the iron used up. It did, however, exhibit different combinations of w and r that were compatible with the consumption of the entire net output ($c = 2\cdot5$). Thus we see that the maximum of w is equal to the maximum of c. What about g and r? In order for the system to increase its scale of production and have a positive g, the production of iron would have to be increased.

Given constant returns we assume that the iron process increases its inputs by 50 per cent and thereby its output by 50 per cent. The physical input requirements of the system then become

$$280 \text{ wheat} + 12 \text{ iron} \to 575 \text{ wheat,}$$
$$180 \text{ wheat} + 12 \text{ iron} \to 30 \text{ iron.}$$

The surplus of this system over its replacement needs is (575 $-460 = 115$) for the wheat process and ($30 - 24 = 6$) for the iron process, or a rate of surplus of 25 per cent in each process. The maximum value of g in this system would then be equal to the maximum profit rate and both are equal to 25 per cent ($115/460 = 6/24 = 1/4$). The following formulation of the system

$$(280 \text{ wheat}) (1+g) + (12 \text{ iron}) (1+g) \to 575 \text{wheat,}$$
$$(180 \text{ wheat}) (1+g) + (12 \text{ iron}) (1+g) \to 30 \text{ iron,}$$

shows that the wheat process needs 280 wheat for replacement and 25 per cent of 280 or 70 wheat for expansion. This leaves $575 - (280 + 70) = 225$ surplus to own wheat requirements which must be exchanged for 12 iron for replacement and (25 per cent of 12) 3 iron for expansion or 15 iron in all.

For the iron process own needs are 12 iron plus (25 per cent of 12) 3 iron or 15 iron out of a gross output of 30 iron. This leaves 15 iron free to be exchanged for wheat requirements of $180 + 45 = 225$, if it is to be able to expand inputs by 25 per cent. Thus, the surplus iron (15) is just equal to the requirements of the wheat process and vice versa. By exchanging at 225 wheat = 15 iron ($p_{iw} = 15$) both can expand at 25 per cent. Rewriting the growth system in terms of wheat values at this exchange rate we have

$$
\begin{aligned}
(280W + 180W) (1+r) &= 575W \\
\underline{(180W + 180W) (1+r)} &= \underline{450W} \\
(460W + 360W) (1+r) &= 1025W
\end{aligned}
$$

which yields $r = 25$ per cent so that in our system $r = g = 0.25$ when $c = w = 0$. It will thus be possible to draw up $c-g$ relations that correspond to and are identical with the $w-r$ relations, given the assumptions about constant returns to scale. The shape of the $c-g$ relations will vary with the technique of production in use and can take either inward- or outward-bulging shapes as well as straight lines [38, 76].

The connection between the $w-r$ and $c-g$ relations will depend on the assumptions we make about savings out of income (wages + profits), for if our system is to satisfy the familiar savings = investment condition, savings out of income must be equal to net investment which will be $g(280$ wheat $+ 12$ iron$) + g(180$ wheat $+ 12$ iron$)$.

If we assume that all wages are spent then all savings come from profits such that, writing s for the proportion of profit saved in our example, $S = sr(280W + 180W) + sr(180W + 180W)$. The value of net physical investment is then $g(280W + 180W) + g(180W + 180W) = I$; or $S = I = g = sr$ which gives the relation between the value of g on the $c-g$ relation and the value of r on the $r-w$ relation. Thus, only when $s = 1$ will $g = r$ and $c = w$, despite the fact that at all values of s the two relations will have identical shape.

The possibility of differing values of c and w (or r and g) highlights a further difficulty in such systems, which can be called composition of output effects [75]. Suppose $r = 0$ and $g = 0.25$, now with $s = 1$ for saving out of wages (which implies $c = 0$). The physical composition of wages (which are now not consumed but saved for investment) must be appropriate to the investment needs of the system, i.e. total wages (115 wheat + 6 iron) are not consumed but invested in expanding the two processes, which is here the case. But, if we had assumed instead that all wages were consumed ($s = 0$) then with $r = 0 = g$, $w = c$. As wheat is the only good that can be consumed the composition of output paid as wages is now inappropriate, for the 6 tons of iron cannot be consumed and it is not needed to increase production with $g = 0$. In such a case production would have to be as in our original system, where only wheat was produced as a net output.

As an intermediate case suppose that profits are partially saved so that $r > g$ and $c > w$ for part of total consumption is now by profit earners as well as wage earners. Such a position would require another (different) combination of final outputs (and thus levels of inputs). In general, then, along any w–r, c–g relation the composition of output and the physical formation of inputs in the system will be different depending on the value of s for both wages and profits [75, 33].

Thus, in a general system one will find two effects at work. First, the value system, symbolised by the w–r relation, will have varying relative prices and values of non-labour means of production as the combinations of w and r vary. Secondly the composition of output will be varying as different values of c and g are examined. When both w–r and c–g are varied together or analysed under different savings assumptions there will be both price variations and variations in the composition of output. As well as the composition of output changing, its value will also be changing, just as the value of the non-labour means of production. (It is for this reason that the chapter worked on the assumptions of a given point in time with only consumption as net output. We now can also see why the relation on p. 68 above is not generally valid for cases where g is positive for q will be different for different g and not necessarily comparable with w, cf. [29 p. 142].)

Thus, if we were to introduce labour into the numerical exercises above, we could no longer take the maximum of the wage as given in physical terms for its composition would be different for different values of s and g. The wage would then always be in value terms and consumption the physical production of consumption goods. These distinctions, of course, do not exist in Sraffa's system for there relations are always worked out for a given point in time with notional differences in w and r (cf. [65]).

4 Conclusions

In Chapter 2 we noted two problems traditionally associated with capital theory, the existence of profit in relation to accumulated capital and the process of accumulation itself. The analysis of Chapter 3 has dealt only with the association of capital and its return in terms of profit, not with explaining the existence of profit or the process of accumulation (thus the use of circulating capital models), problems now most often dealt with in the theory of growth (cf. [50]). The modern debates thus can be seen as emphasising the value aspect of capital theory.

We have already noted that the writers surveyed in Chapter 2 would have accepted the four orthodox propositions only with reservation, but that all evoked an aggregate value-measure of capital when dealing with the economy-wide rate of profits (or interest). Despite their widely varying approaches all writers felt compelled to make an attempt at explaining the magnitude of the ratio of aggregate profit to aggregate capital within their particular framework (save reservation by Wicksell and rejection by Keynes). The results surveyed in Chapter 3, which emerged from Joan Robinson's challenge to the orthodox production function, show that the specification of such an aggregate value of the economy's capital cannot be constructed without prior reference to the profit rate – there can be no value measure of aggregate capital independent of the rate of profits. These results are now accepted by almost all participants in the current debates as offering a formal disproof of the inevitability of the four propositions (or parables as they have been called since Samuelson's defence of them [67]) commonly associated with orthodox capital theory.

For the explanation of the existence of profit, most writers took it as given that an increase in quantity produced would follow an increase in 'capital' and that profit would be paid from this increased quantity. This general idea was justified in a number of ways. Adam Smith talked of the division of labour, Jevons and the Austrians of the increase in output that resulted from the production of intermediate goods which increased the time involved in the production process (a position accepted by Clark, but with the practical reservation that it was not time itself, but the physical goods that time created that were 'physically' responsible for producing the increased final output and resulting profit).

For the Classics, however, profit would be near zero in equilibrium, which meant the stationary state. Positive profit rates could be seen as disequilibrium phenomena which could exist as long as technical progress continued. For the neo-classics this presumption of the profit rate falling to zero was modified as the definition of equilibrium was changed. Clark's creation of a static, imaginary equilibrium at an arbitrary point in time with a given amount of accumulation was radically different from the Classical conception of stationary-state equilibrium. In the static conception the quantities of all factors were given and a position of equilibrium sought from these quantities. Any decline in the profit rate was derived by changing the form and quantity (transmutation) of capital in an imaginary way to find its contribution to production at an imaginary margin. Thus, with given labour a notionally larger stock of capital (but in a form appropriate to the available labour) would have a lower marginal productivity and thus lower rate of profit. But this result is not the end of a process resulting in a position of rest, but an imaginary set of arrangements. While the return to capital is inversely related to the quantity of capital, equilibrium is now consistent with any rate of profit.

It is this result of positive profit rates in imaginary equilibrium that Schumpeter was objecting to when he claimed that in equilibrium under perfect competition the product should be divided between labour and land as original factors, leaving capital with a zero return. He attempted to re-introduce [68] the Classical notion associating positive profit with technical change and disequilibrium.

It was to quell such arguments (as well as to combat Marx) that the production function and its empirical estimation found such wide acceptance, for it purported to show (as Clark emphasised) that capital itself, as a physical object, was physically productive and thus 'deserved' a return. The theory, worked out for an imaginary point in time with given stocks,

87

was also held to apply to actual change through time. Either application required that capital be defined as a measurable and additive quantity. The requirement was different from that of the Classics who needed a quantity of capital to use to identify the ratio of profits to capital in the aggregate. The static approach was founded on the assumptions of given amounts, so that a unique measure of a 'given amount' of capital was required to satisfy the initial assumptions of the specification of a static position; this even before the price of this 'quantity' of capital could be discussed (it is interesting to note that these conditions are close to those that Keynes believed applicable to 'the Theory of the Individual Industry or Firm and of the rewards and the distribution between different uses of a *given* quantity of resources' but wholly inapplicable for the analysis of the economy '*as a whole*' [48 pp. 43, 293]).

Thus there are two basic differences associated with the orthodox and Classical approaches to the analysis of the broad problems of the relation between capital accumulation, the resulting increase in output and the division of the increase between wages and profits. The first is causation. The Classical theory starts from the point of view of production and time to derive the conditions that allow the system to reproduce itself over time. Physical costs of production are the prime determinants of prices. The wage is given by social forces so that distribution is determined by social relations and physical conditions of production (for example diminishing returns to land).

The orthodox or neoclassical approach starts with a given distribution of given quantities at a static point in imaginary time. Utility determines final goods' prices which are then used to impute prices to inputs that are consistent with the final prices and initial supplies (cf. [88 pp. 211 ff.]). The return to each input is then equal to its contribution to production at the margin of its total use. Here wages and profits are determined simultaneously as the marginal contribution of labour and 'capital' (cf. [14] for a discussion of causality in such systems). The use of a given wage in the Classical and given initial quantities in the neoclassical is considered as the crucial point of difference in Garegnani's analysis [23] of the two approaches' analysis of capital. This is simply another way of putting the second difference, the specification of equilibrium; one the result of accumulation over time, the other an imaginary exercise (transmutation) which requires the specification of given quantities to give meaning to the static position (Hicks [41] suggests a distinction between *Fundists* – classic, and *Materialists* – neoclassic).

In a more modern context, the failure of the adequate specification of initial quantities calls into question the foundations of supply and demand in the form of utility and production functions (the formal equivalence of which is stressed in almost all micro texts using indifference and iso-cost curves). All that seems to remain of utility analysis is a weak behavioural assumption implying consistent behaviour in empirically observed market decisions at different points in time (cf. [69]). The production function, aggregate or individual, has not even a weak assumption if taken in value terms, and remains as little more than the statement of a particular physical engineering relationship. The defence of the production function cannot be made on empirical grounds when it has been shown that it rests on invalid logical formulation. Thus theoreticians seek refuge in what is called the full theory of general equilibrium (cf. [32] for an assessment) which is said to require neither utility nor production functions, while others declare that the 'true' neoclassical theory never had anything to do with such concepts as aggregate capital [82, 83]. Chapter 2 allows us to test the veracity of this claim.

There is, however, one aspect of traditional theory that the current debates, in trying to make sense out of the propositions of the static neoclassical theory, tend to overlook. What can we say about the broad problem of accumulating capital leading to an increase in output and declining profit rates? It would be prudent to be sceptical about the applicability of the results of static and stationary-state analysis to the problems of capital accumulation (cf. [63]) and technical progress (cf. [66] on the treatment of technical change), although attempts have been made in this direction [38, 40, 74, 77, 80] and a link between growth and capital theory models can be made through the introduction of a saving relation [76]. Such extensions of the formal models, which must of necessity ignore the problems of uncertainty and expectations that Keynes found crucial, may raise more problems than they pretend to answer. This might suggest that such formal models, set out in terms of aggregate capital, output, prices and so forth, are unsuitable to the question that we want to ask of them. This, of course, is the position that Keynes put forward 40 years ago; the position that Joan Robinson took as understood when she challenged the orthodox theory over its analysis of capital. The results of the current debates seem to confirm Keynes's warning that a sharp line must be drawn between aggregate and partial (static) analysis, as well as between the analysis of a monetary–production economy and an imaginary real barter-exchange economy. On this view the refuge of some orthodox theorists in the analysis of particular positions of short-period equilibrium with specific inputs at a point in time cannot provide an answer to the overall question of the association between capital accumulation and the rate of profit with which capital theorists, Classical and neoclassical, have been traditionally concerned (cf. [25]).

Bibliography

[1] Y. Akyüz, 'Income Distribution, Value of Capital, and Two Notions of the Wage–Profit Trade Off', *Oxford Economic Papers*, XXIV (July 1972).

[2] A. Bhaduri, 'The Concept of the Marginal Productivity of Capital and the Wicksell Effect', *Oxford Economic Papers*, XVIII (Nov 1966).

[3] A. Bhaduri, 'On the Significance of Recent Controversies on Capital Theory: A Marxian View', *Economic Journal*, LXXIX (Sep 1969). Reprinted in [28].

[4] K. Bharadwaj, 'On the Maximum Number of Switches Between Two Production Systems', *Schweizerische Zeitschrift für Volkswirtschaft und Statistik*, CIV, no. 4 (1970).

[5] E. Böhn-Bawerk, *Capital and Interest*, trans. W. Smart (London: Macmillan, 1890).

[6] E. Böhm-Bawerk, *The Positive Theory of Capital*, trans. W. Smart (New York: Stechert, undated).

[7] M. Brown, 'Substitution-Composition Effects, Capital Intensity Uniqueness and Growth', *Economic Journal*, LXXIX (June 1969).

[8] M. Brown, 'Toward an Econometric Accommodation of the Capital-Intensity-Perversity Phenomenon', *Econometrica*, XLI (Sep 1973).

[9] E. Burmeister, 'Neo-Austrian and Alternative Approaches to Capital Theory', *Journal of Economic Literature*, XII (June 1974).

[10] E. Burmeister and S. Turnovsky, 'Capital Deepening Response in an Economy with Heterogeneous Capital Goods', *American Economic Review*, LXII (Dec 1972).

[11] D. G. Champernowne, 'The Production Function and the Theory of Capital: A Comment', *Review of Economic Studies*, XXI (1953–4). Reprinted in [28].

[12] J. B. Clark, *The Distribution of Wealth* (London: Macmillan, 1925).

[13] P. Davidson, *Money and the Real World* (London: Macmillan, 1972).

[14] M. Dobb, *Theories of Value and Distribution* (Cambridge University Press, 1973).

[15] P. H. Douglas, *The Theory of Wages* (New York: Macmillan, 1934).

[16] V. Edelberg, 'The Ricardian Theory of Profit', *Economica*, XIII (Feb 1933).

[17] R. Eisner, 'On Growth Models and the Neoclassical Resurgence', *Economic Journal*, LXVII (Dec 1958).

[18] F. M. Fisher, 'The Existence of Aggregate Production Functions', *Econometrica*, XXXVII (Oct 1969).

[19] F. M. Fisher, 'Aggregate Production Functions and the Explanation of Wages: A simulation experiment', *Review of Economics and Statistics*, LII (Nov 1971).

[20] I. Fisher, *The Nature of Capital and Income* (New York: Macmillan, 1906).

[21] I. Fisher, *The Theory of Interest* (New York: Macmillan, 1930).

[22] L. Gallaway and V. Shukla, 'The Neoclassical Production Function', *American Economic Review*, LXIV (June 1974).

[23] P. Garegnani, *Il Capitale nelle Teorie della Distribuzione* (Milan: Giuffre, 1960).

[24] P. Garegnani, 'Heterogeneous Capital, the Production Function and the Theory of Distribution', *Review of Economic Studies*, XXXVII (July 1970).

[25] P. Garegnani, 'Comment' in [53].

[26] P. D. Groenewegen, 'Three Notes on Ricardo's Theory of Value and Distribution', *Australian Economic Papers*, XI (June 1972).

[27] G. C. Harcourt, 'Some Cambridge Controversies in the Theory of Capital', *Journal of Economic Literature*, VII (June 1969).

[28] G. C. Harcourt and W. F. Laing, *Capital and Growth* (Harmondsworth: Penguin, 1971).

[29] G. C. Harcourt, *Some Cambridge Controversies in the Theory of Capital* (Cambridge University Press, 1972).

[30] G. C. Harcourt and V. G. Massaro, 'A Note on Mr Sraffa's Sub-systems', *Economic Journal*, LXXIV (Sep 1964).

[31] G. C. Harcourt and A. Asimakopoulos, 'Proportionality and the Neoclassical Parables', *Southern Economic Journal*, XL (Jan 1974).

[32] G. C. Harcourt, 'The Cambridge Controversies: The Afterglow', in *Contemporary Issues in Economics*, ed. M. Parkin and A. R. Nobay (Manchester University Press, 1975).

[33] D. J. Harris, 'Capital, Distribution and the Aggregate Production Function', *American Economic Review*, LXIII (Mar 1973).

[34] R. F. Harrod, *Towards a Dynamic Economics* (London: Macmillan, 1948).

[35] F. A. Hayek, 'The Mythology of Capital', *Quarterly Journal of Economics*, L (Feb 1936).

[36] D. F. Heathfield, *Production Functions* (London: Macmillan, 1971).

[37] J. R. Hicks, *The Theory of Wages* (London: Macmillan, 1932).

[38] J. R. Hicks, *Capital and Growth* (Oxford University Press, 1965).

[39] J. R. Hicks, 'A Neo-Austrian Growth Theory', *Economic Journal*, LXXX (June 1970).

[40] J. R. Hicks, *Capital and Time* (Oxford: Clarendon Press, 1973).

[41] J. R. Hicks, 'Capital Controversies: Ancient and Modern', *American Economic Review*, LXIV (May 1974).

[42] J. Hirshleifer, *Investment, Interest and Capital* (Englewood Cliffs, N.J.: Prentice-Hall, 1970).

[43] W. S. Jevons, *The Theory of Political Economy* (Harmondsworth: Penguin, 1970).

[44] R. F. Kahn and D. G. Champernowne, 'The Value of Invested Capital', in [61].

[45] N. Kaldor, *Essays in Value and Distribution* (London: Duckworth, 1960).

[46] M. Kalecki, *Selected Essays on the Dynamics of the Capitalist Economy* (Cambridge University Press, 1971).

[47] J. M. Keynes, *A Treatise on Money* (London: Macmillan, 1930).

[48] J. M. Keynes, *The General Theory of Employment, Interest and Money* (London: Macmillan, 1936).

[49] F. M. Knight, 'Capital and Interest', in *Readings in the Theory of Income Distribution* (Philadelphia: Blakiston, 1949).

[50] J. A. Kregel, *Theory of Economic Growth* (London: Macmillan, 1972).

[51] D. Laibman and E. J. Nell, 'Reswitching, Wicksell Effects and the Neoclassical Production Function', mimeo. (New York, 1975).

[52] D. Levhari, 'A Nonsubstitution Theorem and the Switching of Techniques', *Quarterly Journal of Economics*, LXXIX (Feb 1965).

[53] J. A. Mirrlees and N. H. Stern, *Models of Growth* (London: Macmillan, 1973).

[54] G. Moore, *Laws of Wages, An Essay in Statistical Economics* (New York: Macmillan, 1911).

[55] D. M. Nuti, 'Capitalism, Socialism and Steady Growth', *Economic Journal*, LXXX (Mar 1970). Reprinted in [28].

[56] 'Paradoxes in Capital Theory: A Symposium', *Quarterly Journal of Economics*, LXXX (Nov 1966).

[57] L. L. Pasinetti, 'Switches of Technique and the "Rate of Return" in Capital Theory', *Economic Journal*, LXXIX (Sep 1969). Reprinted in [28].

[58] D. Ricardo, *Principles of Political Economy and Taxation*, ed. P. Sraffa (Cambridge University Press, 1951).

[59] Joan Robinson, *The Rate of Interest and Other Essays* (London: Macmillan, 1952).

[60] Joan Robinson, 'The Production Function and the Theory of Capital', *Review of Economic Studies*, XXI (1953–4). Reprinted in [28].

[61] Joan Robinson, *The Accumulation of Capital* (London: Macmillan, 1956).

[62] Joan Robinson and K. A. Naqvi, 'The Badly-Behaved Production Function', *Quarterly Journal of Economics*, LXXXI (Nov 1967).

[63] Joan Robinson, 'The Unimportance of Reswitching', *Quarterly Journal of Economics*, LXXXIX (Feb 1975).

[64] A. Roncaglia, 'Labour-power, Subsistence Wage and the Rate of Wages', *Australian Economic Papers*, XIII (June 1974).

[65] A. Roncaglia, *Sraffa e la Teoria dei Prezzi* (Rome: Laterza, 1975).

[66] T. K. Rymes, *Capital and Technical Change* (Cambridge University Press, 1971).

[67] P. A. Samuelson, 'Parable and Realism in Capital Theory: The Surrogate Production Function', *Review of Economic Studies*, XXIX (June 1962). Reprinted in [28].

[68] J. A. Schumpeter, *Theory of Economic Development*, trans. R. Opie (New York: Oxford University Press, 1961).

[69] A. K. Sen, 'Behaviour and the Concept of Preference', *Economica*, XL (Aug 1973).

[70] A. Shaik, 'Laws of Production and the Laws of Algebra: The Humbug Production Function', *Review of Economics and Statistics*, LVI (Feb 1974).

[71] A. Smith, *The Wealth of Nations*, ed. McCulloch (Edinburgh: Black & Tait, 1838).

[72] R. M. Solow, 'The Production Function and the Theory of Capital', *Review of Economic Studies*, XXVIII (1955-6).

[73] R. M. Solow, *Capital Theory and the Rate of Return* (Amsterdam: North-Holland, 1963). Partially reprinted in [28].

[74] R. M. Solow, 'The Interest Rate and the Transition between Techniques', in *Socialism, Capitalism and Steady Growth*, ed. C. H. Feinstein (Cambridge University Press, 1967).

[75] L. Spaventa, 'Realism Without Parables in Capital Theory', in *Recherches récentes sur la fonction de production* (Namur: CERUNA, 1968).

[76] L. Spaventa, 'Rate of Profit, Rate of Growth and Capital Intensity in a Simple Growth Model', *Oxford Economic Papers*, XXII (July 1970).

[77] L. Spaventa, 'Notes on Problems of Transitions between Techniques', in [53].

[78] P. Sraffa, *Production of Commodities By Means of Commodities* (Cambridge University Press, 1960); ch. 6 partially reprinted in [28].

[79] I. Steedman, 'Jevons's Theory of Capital and Interest', *Manchester School*, XL (Mar 1972).

[80] I. Steedman and J. S. Metcalfe, 'A Note of the "Gain from Trade" ', *Economic Record*, L (Dec 1974).

[81] I. Steedman, 'Fixed Capital and the Surrogate Production Function', mimeo. (Manchester, 1975).

[82] J. E. Stiglitz, 'The Cambridge–Cambridge Controversy in the Theory of Capital', *Journal of Political Economy*, LXXXII (July–Aug 1974).

[83] J. E. Stiglitz, 'The Badly Behaved Economy with the Well-Behaved Production Function', and 'Recurrence of Techniques in a Dynamic Economy', in [53].

[84] Th. van de Klundert and A. van Schaik, 'Durable Capital and Economic Growth', *de Economist*, CXXII (May–June 1974).

[85] L. Walras, *Elements of Pure Economics*, trans. W. Jaffe (London: Unwin, 1954).

[86] K. Wicksell, *Value, Capital and Rent*, trans. S. Frowein (New York: Kelley, 1970).

[87] K. Wicksell, *Lectures in Political Economy*, vol. I, trans. E. Classen (London: Routledge & Kegan Paul, 1934).

[88] P. Wicksteed, *An Essay on the Co-ordination of the Laws of Distribution* (London: Macmillan, 1894).